LEFT *of*
LEADERSHIP

LEFT *of*
LEADERSHIP

The Prequel to Success

SCOTT H. STALKER

LEFT OF LEADERSHIP
The Prequel to Success
by Scott H. Stalker

First Edition
Copyright © 2025

Published by
Munn Avenue Press
300 Main Street, Ste 21
Madison, NJ 07940
MunnAvenuePress.com

For permission requests, contact MunnAvenuePress.com

Paperback ISBN: 978-1-960299-90-1
Hardcover ISBN: 978-1-960299-91-8

Printed in the United States of America

To my wife, Malerie Stalker—

*You are my love, the leader of our family,
and the unwavering center of our lives. Your strength, grace,
and devotion as the mother of our daughters—Olivia,
Grace, and Scarlett—have shaped our home and grounded
our future. You are the most precious person in my life,
and nothing I do is possible without you.*

*And to Lieutenant General Vincent R. Stewart,
United States Marine Corps (Retired)—*

*Your example of leadership, mentorship, and integrity
made a lasting impact on me and so many others. I would
not be in the position to write this book without your
influence. You lived E Pluribus Unum and embodied
Semper Fidelis in every way. Thank you, Sir. May your
legacy live on through those you led.*

— CONTENTS —

— FOREWORD —

I suspect many of you are like me—one of the 20,000 followers of Scott Stalker on LinkedIn or Facebook. Nearly every day, Scott shares with his legion of readers the foundational principles that empower us to lead better, learn better, and live better. From his engaging writing style to his humor and powerful messaging, Scott is a gifted communicator who attracts new followers daily.

But before Scott became a social media phenomenon, he was a leader in the United States Marine Corps and across our Joint Force. I know him well, having worked closely with him at U.S. Cyber Command and the National Security Agency—two of the four national security organizations where he served as the senior enlisted leader. His leadership influence reached across all levels: superiors, peers, and subordinates alike.

In his first book, *Left of Leadership*, Scott shares his core idea about the most essential quality of any organization or team. Repurposing the term "left of boom"—coined during the War on Terrorism to describe efforts to prevent IED attacks by disrupting networks well before detonation—Scott cultivates a similar mindset: you must prepare well before you are ever officially "in charge." Through stories and reflections, he offers a clear thesis—leadership isn't about titles, roles, or formal authority. It's about impact, intent, and integrity.

In a crowded field of leadership books, why does this one matter? I offer three reasons:

First, every organization needs leaders who can provide vision, direction, and motivation. Scott's focus on mastering fundamentals—clear communication, critical thinking, sound decision-making, emotional intelligence, and self-discipline—offers firsthand lessons for building a leadership baseline.

Second, in an era where we're increasingly disconnected—through screens, dispersed teams, and AI-generated content—Scott returns us to the heart of leadership: people. Whether it's remembering names (just ask his daughters!), learning someone's story before trying to lead them, or redefining love in leadership as accountability, care, and compassion—he reminds us leadership is, at its core, human.

Finally, Scott's own journey—from humble beginnings to senior enlisted leadership—demonstrates that leaders are not born, but built. Built through education, mentorship, adversity, and deliberate practice. His memorable quips, or what I call "Stalker-isms," reinforce that truth: "Success is rented, and rent is due every day."

As a lifelong student of leadership, I commend *Left of Leadership* to your personal library. We live in uncertain times—emerging threats abroad, eroding trust in institutions, and technologies that both empower and endanger. Yet in the face of uncertainty, one thing remains constant: leadership matters. I hope this book adds to your leadership journey. I thank each of you who lead with purpose—and Scott, for sharing his journey so candidly.

Paul M. Nakasone
General, U.S. Army (Ret.)
White Bear Lake, Minnesota
May 25, 2025

"Leadership and learning
are indispensable to each other."
— John F. Kennedy

— 1 —

THE LEADERSHIP LABYRINTH: NAVIGATING THE UNKNOWN

I never thought I'd be writing a book about leadership. If you had told that skinny kid from New Hampshire who was stealing hood ornaments off cars that he'd one day become the senior enlisted leader for multiple intelligence agencies and defense organizations, he would have laughed in your face. But here we are.

Let me paint you a picture of where this journey began. No silver spoons or straight paths here. Just a kid with too much unsupervised time, not enough structure, and a talent for finding trouble. I'd skip school to play basketball, shoplift from 7-Eleven, and do pretty much anything to avoid being at home where my parents were dealing with their own demons of abuse and addiction. I didn't have a role model, a mentor, or even a clear example of what leadership looked like. I had chaos. I had survival.

School was mind-numbingly boring, so I convinced my parents to let me graduate early at seventeen. Then I did what seemed like the most extreme thing possible at the time—I joined the Marine Corps. My sisters were just kids—eleven and fourteen—and I don't think they fully understood what I was doing. I didn't either, not really. There were no heartfelt send-offs, no hugs at the door, and no final family dinner. My sisters didn't say goodbye because they didn't know I wasn't coming back . . . and maybe I didn't either. That morning felt like any other day, except it wasn't. It was the end of one life and the beginning of another. My mom was too busy with her friends to say goodbye. My dad managed a handshake and a "Good luck." I got in the car with my recruiter, and it was off to boot camp and the infamous Marine Corps bus I had to quickly "get off" of.

That chapter closed behind me, silent and unceremonious. Three days into boot camp, as I stood there having pissed my pants, I seriously questioned all my life choices. That was my first real lesson in leadership: You can't fake preparation. Not with your body, not with your mind.

But here's where it gets interesting. I graduated boot camp and got selected for intelligence school based on my test scores. I showed up to Intel school with more arrogance than a tech billionaire, thinking I was too smart to need to study. The result? I graduated dead last in my class.

Dead. Last.

This isn't exactly the inspirational story you were expecting, is it? Good. Because this book isn't about following some perfect path to leadership. It's about the messy, humbling work that happens long before you ever get a fancy title or corner office.

The modern workplace, whether military or civilian, is struggling with how to develop real leaders. We're great at promoting people into management positions and giving them impressive titles. But titles are fleeting. The moment you leave, they evaporate. Too many people cling to who they were instead of growing into who they could be.

Meanwhile, technology is rapidly changing how we work. Artificial Intelligence, virtual workplaces, digital everything. These are incredible tools, but they're just that—tools. They don't automatically make you a leader. In fact, in some ways, they make authentic leadership harder to develop.

I see it everywhere—people trying to skip the foundational work of leadership. They want to sell you the shiny solution before building trust. They want to manage via email instead of looking people in the eye. They want authority without doing the work to earn real influence.

Here's what I've learned in over 30 years of service: The best leaders I've ever had weren't necessarily the ones making the dramatic combat decisions. They were the ones who took the time to ask, "How's your family?" and meant it. They were the ones who remembered names, noticed details, and genuinely cared about their people.

I'll never forget what one of my mentors told me: "If somebody truly cares about me, I'll run through fire for them." That's not hyperbole in the Marines. The kind of leadership that inspires that level of trust and loyalty? It doesn't come from a title. It comes from putting in the work long before you're ever in charge.

This book is about the work that happens *before* the title, *before* the authority, and *before* you're ever officially "in charge." Left of Leadership is the space where real leadership begins.

What Does "Left of Leadership" Really Mean?

In military operations, we use the term "Left of Boom" to describe everything that must happen before a kinetic strike, explosive event, or offensive military action takes place. The "boom" is the event. This mindset shaped how we approached threats like IEDs in Iraq and Afghanistan—focusing not just on response, but on readiness before the moment of impact. Everything to the left of it is preparation: intelligence gathering, surveillance, planning, rehearsals, and drills.

Left of Leadership follows the same principle. It's the leadership equivalent of Left of Boom. In military operations, you don't wait for the explosion to react, you prepare far in advance to prevent or mitigate the damage. The same is true for leadership; you don't wait until you're put in charge to start leading. You start preparing now, long before the moment of impact.

And in the world of space operations—NASA, SpaceX, and the U.S. Space Force—we talk about being "Left of Launch." That phrase refers to all the preparation that happens before a rocket ever leaves the ground: trajectory analysis, risk assessments, system redundancy checks, simulations, and rehearsals. No one shows up on launch day and wings it. It's months—sometimes years—of precise, methodical planning to ensure that once the countdown hits zero, everything is ready to perform under pressure.

Left of Leadership works the same way. It's the mindset that says: I don't need a title to take ownership. I don't need a promotion to add value. I don't need permission to lead by example. It's about doing the reps before the mission starts, because by the time everyone's watching, it's too late to get ready.

It's about preparing before you step into the role, long before the title is conferred or the authority granted. It's about the internal work: the discipline, mindset, character, and relationships you build now so that when the time comes, you're not just ready, you're already leading.

I want to be crystal clear about this. Leadership doesn't begin when you get a title. It begins with preparation. It begins with reflection. It begins with choices you make when no one's watching.

Left of Leadership means four things:

1. **Own your mindset** – Learn to control your thoughts before they control you.

2. **Master your habits** – Show up early. Take notes. Keep promises. Do the hard things first.

3. **Build unshakable trust** – People don't follow titles; they follow people they believe in.

4. **Develop invisible influence** – Cultivate the kind of leadership that shows up before your nameplate does.

You can call it leadership insurance. You're not just reacting; you're preparing so well, so consistently that when the moment comes, you've already earned your place.

Leadership doesn't begin with a promotion.
It begins with preparation.

I wish I'd had this book when I was that arrogant kid in Intel school. But the truth is, I probably wouldn't have read it. I had to learn these lessons the hard way. My hope is that by sharing them now, I can help you navigate this labyrinth with a bit more wisdom than I had.

The path to real leadership isn't a straight line. It's a labyrinth of challenges, setbacks, and opportunities for growth. But here's what I know for sure: The work you put in Left of Leadership—the character you build, the relationships you forge, the trust you earn—that's what determines whether people will follow you because they have to, or because they want to.

Let's begin.

The Power of Preparation

One of the first lessons I learned about leadership came through preparation—or, more accurately, my complete lack of it. After graduating last in my class at Intel school, I started to understand that success isn't about natural talent or intelligence. It's about the work you put in before the moment of truth.

Preparation is how you cheat time. We all get the same 24 hours. But how you use the hours before determines how effectively you can use the hours ahead. When I'm prepping for a speech, I study the audience. I visualize the performance. I rehearse like it's a stand-up routine. I watch great speakers the way athletes watch game films.

Here's my Three-Part Prep Protocol:

- **Understand the mission:** What's the goal? Why does it matter?

- **Know the audience:** What do they value? What language will land?
- **Visualize the win:** What does a home run look like? See it before you swing.

Preparation isn't just about big moments. It's about the small daily habits that compound over time. In our house with three young kids, my wife and I prep for the next day every night—not just for us, but to help them too. School bags packed, lunches made, clothes laid out. It's not about control; it's about minimizing morning chaos and setting our whole family up for success. Preparation reduces friction. It frees up focus. It lets us start the day with intention instead of reaction.

"Preparation," I tell my teams, "is the only way I know to cheat the hours in a day."

—

One of the earliest memories I have of applying this principle took place back in 1993, just before I graduated from intelligence school. I was tasked with giving a briefing to none other than Lieutenant General Paul Van Riper, a legendary Marine who had just implemented major changes to Marine Corps intelligence doctrine, known as the Van Riper Plan. It was a simple brief, really—just a weather overview before we moved into the standard WET format: weather, enemy, terrain. But simple doesn't mean easy when you're eighteen, in uniform, and standing in front of a man who looked like he wanted to rip your head off just for breathing too loud. I was prepared. I knew my material. But I still shook in my boots.

I felt nervous. The briefing wasn't just about information; it was about delivery, posture, tone. And that moment taught me something crucial: Preparation doesn't erase fear, it gives you a foundation to stand on when fear shows up. I gave the brief. It wasn't perfect. But it landed. And his questions afterward helped me learn and improve. That small, intimidating moment started something: I began the journey of becoming the kind of leader who doesn't freeze under pressure because of having already put in the work Left of Leadership.

Think about video games for a minute. Everyone wants to be a warrior in combat, executing the perfect mission. You get to be the sniper, the SEAL, the Marine, the Special Forces hero charging into the fight. It's instant action, instant power, and instant gratification. But what those games never show—because it wouldn't sell—is the years of work it takes to become that kind of warrior in real life.

No one picks up a controller and sees the endless ruck marches, the late-night study sessions, the reps on the range, the sleepless nights on post, the failures, the do-overs, the personal discipline. That's the real stuff. That's the grind that makes the mission possible. Games skip straight to the glory, but leadership doesn't work that way.

Leadership is forged in the exact same way success in combat is earned, long before anyone pulls the trigger. It's the quiet preparation, the unseen effort, the repetition no one applauds. That's where real leaders are built.

This level of preparation might seem excessive to some. But I've learned that the difference between good and great often comes down to what happens left of the moment, all the unglamorous work that nobody sees.

Most leadership books jump straight to the combat phase: Here's how to manage a team, how to make tough decisions, how to handle a crisis. But they skip over all the foundational work that needs to happen first. That's like trying to play the final level without going through the training missions.

I see this mistake all the time in the modern workforce. People get promoted into management positions without having developed the underlying skills and habits that make leadership possible. They have the title, but they haven't done the preparation. It's like being handed a weapon without going through basic training first.

Building Character Before Command

A lot of discussions about character and values in leadership dive straight into organized religion or corporate ethics statements. But in my experience, character isn't about checking boxes or following a prescribed set of rules. It's about finding your moral compass and staying true to it, even when—especially when—nobody's watching.

I learned this lesson in an unexpected place—a Catholic church in my hometown when I was fourteen. I was riding my bike one Tuesday afternoon, probably killing time to avoid going home, when I wandered into the church. Father Castro found me sitting there and did something that would change my life. He actually took the time to talk to me.

"Tell me about yourself, son," he said. That simple act of genuine interest led to him introducing me to a family that went to Mass every Saturday at 5 p.m. They offered to pick me up each week, and suddenly, I had structure in my life for the first time. I had something to look forward to, something consistent in a world that felt anything but.

I dove in completely; that's just how I'm wired. I either do something or I don't. I went through the catechism course as a teenager, got confirmed at sixteen, and for a while, I seriously considered becoming a priest. My parents didn't come to any of it; they didn't participate in any way, but that almost made it more meaningful. This was something I had chosen for myself.

What drew me to Catholicism wasn't blind faith; I needed to do deep research, to get beyond what everyone was telling me and understand the foundations. What grabbed me most was learning about how Christ gave the keys to Saint Peter, establishing a lineage that could be traced all the way back to him. As someone whose life had lacked structure and consistency, that unbroken chain of tradition meant something to me.

Eventually, my calling to join the Marine Corps proved stronger than my calling to the priesthood. But the lessons I learned during that time about character, discipline, and having something to believe in have shaped my entire approach to leadership.

Here's what I've learned: Being kind, being ethical, and showing integrity aren't things you do because some rule book tells you to. You do them because they're the right thing to do. Because there's enough winning available for all of us. Success doesn't have to come at someone else's expense.

This shows up in small ways every day. Recently, I was driving my daughters to their leadership charter school, and I watched a parent pull into a handicap spot who clearly didn't need it. They were probably thinking, "I'm just going to be quick" or "Nobody else is using it right now." But character isn't about what's convenient— it's about what's right.

I tell my girls all the time that the audio has to match the video. In other words, your actions have to align with your words. When I first started watching martial arts movies in the '80s, I couldn't understand why Bruce Lee's lips didn't match what he was saying. I didn't know about dubbing back then. But it taught me something important: When things don't line up, when what someone's saying doesn't match what they're doing, people notice.

This is especially crucial in leadership. You can talk about values all day long, but if you take shortcuts when nobody's looking, if you bend the rules when it's convenient, your team will see it. They might not say anything, but they'll notice. And more importantly, they'll remember.

That's why character must come before leadership. You have to figure out what you stand for and practice living it consistently, long before you're in a position where others are looking to you for guidance. Because once you're in that position, it's too late to start developing character. Your habits, good and bad, will already be set.

I think about that church sometimes, about how different my life might have been if Father Castro hadn't taken the time to talk to me on a random Tuesday afternoon. It reminds me that character isn't just about following rules, it's about how we treat people, especially when there's nothing in it for us. That's the kind of leader I strive to be and the kind of leader this world desperately needs more of.

My faith is something I keep to myself these days. That's a choice I've made, but I can say without hesitation that this brief encounter had a profound impact on me. And it wasn't just what Father Castro said—it was how he carried himself. How he listened. How he gave me his full attention like I actually mattered. That simple act of presence and care left a mark on me that I still carry. It taught me that leadership doesn't always look like command; sometimes it looks like quiet attention and showing up when no one else does.

Building Trust Before Authority

You can't sell someone a shiny object without trust. Yet I watch people try to do exactly that every day. They attempt to lead without first building relationships and try to influence without first establishing trust.

Trust doesn't come from a handbook. It comes from shared experiences. From remembering someone's name. From asking how their kids are doing. From following through. People will run through fire for leaders who show they care. But you can't fake it. Your team knows when your interest is genuine and when it's transactional.

Let me give you a simple example from my own life. I don't shop at Lowe's or Walmart for my hardware needs. Instead, I go to the Ace Hardware store down the street, where they know my name. Yes, I probably pay a little more. But there's real value in walking in and hearing, "Hey Scott, how's everyone doing?"

Remember the TV show *Cheers*? Norm didn't go there because they had the best beer in Boston. He went there because it was where everybody knew his name. There's profound wisdom in that simple concept. When people feel known, when they feel valued as individuals rather than just customers or employees, everything changes.

I see this play out at the highest levels of leadership. Take my relationship with Retired Army Four-Star General Paul Nakasone, the former director of the National Security Agency and Commander of U.S. Cyber Command. When he calls me now, he doesn't just dive into business. He asks about my wife Malerie and our girls. Not because there's some checklist in his head saying, "Ask about family," but because he genuinely cares. That's the kind of leader people will storm through a brick wall for.

This kind of relationship-building isn't just beneficial, it's fundamental to effective leadership. Many of my speaking engagements today result directly from introductions made by trusted teammates who believe in what I bring to the table.

They trust me because I've built professional relationships with them over time. All of these things must happen Left of Leadership, before you're ever in a position of authority.

But here's the catch: You can't fake it. People can smell inauthentic interest a mile away. When we go out to dinner, I play a game with my daughters. I tell them that if they can remember their server's name by the end of the meal, I will give them each a dollar. I believe this 'game' is about teaching them that every person deserves to be seen, acknowledged, and treated with respect.

One of the best lessons I've learned about trust came from working with senior military leaders. At U.S. Space Command, I once had to approach a frustrated admiral with context that clarified our commander's intent. I had no authority to direct him, but I had influence—because we had built trust.

I didn't come to him to tell him what to do, or how to do it. That wasn't my role. I came to listen first. To understand his frustration, his challenges, and his perspective. Only after he'd said his piece did I share the bigger picture—what our commander's end state was and how this work fit into that larger mission. I wasn't there to give orders. I was there to connect the dots, bridge the gap, and help him see that he wasn't being left out—he was essential.

That's what trust allows you to do. You can speak into tension because you've already invested in the relationship. You can influence without authority. And you can move the mission forward without pulling rank.

Trust can't be retrofitted. It is built before the crisis. Left of Leadership.

This is what I mean when I talk about the work that must happen Left of Leadership. Building relationships and trust isn't something you can do after you get the position. It has to happen before—in all the small moments, the daily interactions, the times when nobody's watching.

Think about your own workplace. Who are the people you truly trust? I bet they earned that trust long before they had any authority over you. They probably earned it through consistent actions, genuine interest, and demonstrated integrity.

That's why I get frustrated when I see leadership development programs that focus solely on decision-making skills or management techniques. Those things matter, but they're useless without a foundation of trust. It's like trying to build a house starting with the roof.

I see this problem getting worse in our increasingly virtual world. We think we can build relationships through email or manage teams through Zoom. And while these tools are valuable, they can't replace the fundamental human need for genuine connection.

I have witnessed my single friends struggling with dating apps. The same principle applies here: Technology can facilitate connections but it can't create them. That takes human effort, genuine interest, and time.

When I consult with organizations now, I often ask their leaders a simple question: "If I asked your team about you, what would they say?" Not about your technical skills or your management style, but about you as a person. Do they feel known by you? Do they trust you? Because if they don't, all the authority in the world won't make you an effective leader.

The good news is that building trust isn't complicated. It doesn't require special skills or advanced degrees. It just requires genuine interest in people and the willingness to consistently demonstrate that interest through your actions. Remember names. Ask questions. Follow up. Show up when it matters.

These might seem like small things, but they're the foundation on which everything else is built. Because at the end of the day, people don't follow titles, they follow people they trust.

Preserving the Human Touch in a Digital Age

Let me be clear: I'm not anti-technology. Hell, I earned my Master of Science in Cybersecurity and served as the Command Senior Enlisted Leader for U.S. Cyber Command and the National Security Agency. I understand technology and the critical role it plays. I use AI tools, appreciate virtual workplaces, and value the efficiency tech provides. But after three decades of leadership experience, I've learned that technology is a tool, not a panacea—especially when it comes to leadership. I've seen how it can make us faster, more precise, and more capable. But leadership is about human beings. And people don't follow code. They follow connection.

Here's what I see happening in today's workforce: We're getting incredibly efficient at processes while simultaneously losing touch with people. Organizations invest millions in digital transformation but forget to invest in human connection. We're building virtual teams without understanding how to build virtual trust.

Think about how we work now. A virtual workplace doesn't require as much human interaction, and that's fine . . . until it isn't. Until you need someone to go above and beyond their job description. Until you need innovation that only comes from collaboration. Until you need the kind of loyalty that makes someone willing to run through fire for the team.

Back to the dating app analogy. Now, I know there are times it works, but for a lot of people, it ends up feeling like a soul-destroying experience. You look at someone's profile for 1.5 seconds, and if you're not instantly attracted, you swipe away. Think about what's lost there. How many potential connections never happen because we've removed the human element?

The same thing happens in leadership. We think we can manage through emails, lead through text messages, and build culture through virtual meetings. But real leadership—the kind that inspires people to excel, to innovate, to persist through challenges—requires human connection.

Remember what I said earlier about going to the local Ace Hardware store instead of the big box stores? In a world of automated checkouts and online ordering, I'll gladly pay a little more to do business with people who know my name. It's not nostalgia, it's recognition that human connection has real value.

This is especially crucial as artificial intelligence becomes more prevalent in our workplaces. Yes, AI can help us be more efficient.

Yes, it can automate routine tasks. Yes, it can even help us make better decisions. But it can't replace the fundamental human elements of leadership:

- It can't show genuine care for someone's well-being
- It can't build trust through consistent actions over time
- It can't inspire someone to push beyond their perceived limits
- It can't create the kind of loyalty that defines great teams

I see this play out at the highest levels of leadership. Some of the best leaders I've known weren't necessarily the ones making the dramatic combat decisions. They were the ones who took the time to ask, "Scott, how are you doing? How are Malerie and the kids?" And they meant it.

That's why, even as technology advances, the fundamentals of leadership remain remarkably consistent. People still need to feel valued. They still need to feel connected. They still need to trust their leaders. These aren't soft skills, they're essential requirements for effective leadership.

I've watched teams collapse because leaders tried to automate their presence. Emails instead of conversations. Texts instead of check-ins. Metrics instead of mentorship. Don't get me wrong—tools matter. But tools don't lead people. People lead people. Dale Carnegie said it nearly a century ago, and it's still true: "You can make more friends in two months by being interested in other people than in two years by trying to get people interested in you." That's not fluff. That's a tactical advantage in leadership. Human connection is an asset—one that compounds when built early, Left of Leadership.

A video call will never replace a handshake. A Slack message won't replace standing next to someone in a moment that matters. Leadership is a contact sport—it's felt. And the leaders who win in a digital world will be the ones who know when to close the laptop and look someone in the eyes.

It's not about rejecting technology. It's about using it to amplify your leadership, not replace it. Human connection is your edge. Don't outsource it.

The challenge for aspiring leaders today is to embrace technology without losing humanity. To use digital tools while maintaining human connections. To become more efficient without becoming less personal.

Here's what I tell young leaders: If you want to truly separate yourself in today's workplace, master the human element. Have character. Remember names. Show genuine interest in people. In a world where everyone is focused on technical skills and digital transformation, these "old-school" leadership qualities become even more valuable.

Because here's the truth: While we'll all be using AI and other advanced technologies, we still need the human touch. We still need leaders who can look people in the eye (even through a screen), who can build trust, and who can inspire others to excel.

The most effective leaders in the digital age will be those who can bridge both worlds—who can leverage technology while maintaining genuine human connections. We must understand that while AI can help us make better decisions, it can't make us better leaders. That still requires the human work: the preparation, character-building, and relationship development that happens Left of Leadership.

You can see this truth echoed in the first SOF Truth: *Humans are more important than hardware.* And while today's missions often rely just as heavily on software, sensors, and AI, that truth still holds. Maybe now more than ever. Because the tech can only go so far without a human who understands the mission, cares about the people, and leads with clarity.

The first Chief Master Sergeant of the Space Force, Roger Towberman, put it plainly and powerfully. He called it the First Space Truth: *Our most important weapon system lives and breathes.* That's not just a slogan, that's a reality. That's the human sitting at the console, the junior enlisted monitoring the feed, the NCO making the call under pressure. That's you.

Left of Leadership is about investing in that weapon system early—before the mission, before the pressure, before the title. Human connection, just like technical competence, is something you train for. And when the time comes, it shows.

As we wrap up this chapter, remember this: Leadership isn't about the tools you use, it's about the trust you build. It's not about the technology you master, it's about the people you develop. And most importantly, it's not about the title you hold, it's about the impact you have on others.

That's what this book is about. Not just how to become a leader, but how to do the fundamental human work that makes real leadership possible. Because in an increasingly digital world, the human element of leadership isn't becoming less important, it's becoming essential.

Looking Ahead

As we move into Chapter 2, we'll explore how love and compassion form the foundation of effective leadership. This might seem counterintuitive, especially coming from a Marine. But as you'll see, the ability to genuinely care for others, to lead with both head and heart, is what separates good leaders from great ones.

The skills and habits we've discussed in this chapter—preparation, character, relationship-building, and maintaining human connection—all serve as building blocks for what comes next. Because once you understand that true leadership comes from a place of genuine care and concern for others, everything else falls into place.

Get ready to challenge your assumptions about what makes a leader effective.

CHAPTER TAKEAWAYS

- **Preparation is your power:** You can't control outcomes, but you can always control your readiness.
- **Habits matter more than hype:** Daily consistency is more important than motivational bursts.
- **Trust beats authority:** Build it before you need it.
- **Character compounds:** The right choices add up, quietly.
- **Stay human:** In a tech-heavy world, human leadership will be the rarest and most powerful kind.

Action Steps

1. **Evening prep routine:** Set your next day up before bed.
2. **Identify your three core values:** Write them. Live them.
3. **Track trust moments:** Each day, note one thing you did to build trust.
4. **Practice presence:** One human interaction a day with no phone, no distraction.
5. **Create a "prep audit":** List five areas of your life where better preparation could change the outcome.

This is the start of your leadership journey. Left of Leadership is where it begins. Let's keep going.

"People don't care how much you know
until they know how much you care."
– Theodore Roosevelt

– 2 –

LEADING WITH LOVE

Love doesn't usually make it into leadership manuals. But it should. Because the best leaders I've ever followed didn't just push me, they cared about me. And they proved it.

A recent call from Lieutenant General Vince Stewart's widow, Phyllis, stirred memories that deepened my understanding of true leadership. The General's passing, not long ago, left behind a profound legacy—one that continues to shape my views on leadership and authority. I learned of his passing just a day after speaking with him, during which he had agreed to be my 'retiring officer' (when someone retires in the military a commissioned officer has to do the retiring. I wanted Lt. General Vince Stewart to be the one to speak at my ceremony). Months after his passing, I found myself in a state of numb disbelief, almost as if watching from outside my own body, as I attended his funeral service at Arlington National Cemetery.

We spent years together, traveling to more than twenty countries, sharing countless meals, laughter, tears, and the occasional tough heart-to-heart discussion. During his memorial and funeral, my mind continually drifted back to those shared experiences. Though it was a time meant for mourning, I found myself gently smiling, lost in memories of the extraordinary journey we had together.

The concept of a Marine discussing love and leadership might seem incongruous at first. The Marine Corps, with our deep-rooted traditions and ironclad customs, operates almost like a sacred order, though I mean that in the most respectful sense. During our annual Marine Corps Birthday Ball, which is filled with tradition, we have the reading of our 13th Commandant General John A. Lejeune's message, where during that message he calls upon us to be a worthy successor. Reading the "worthy successors" statement is required as a reminder of our duty to honor and build upon the foundation our predecessors established.

Yet true worth sometimes demands breaking with tradition, as General Stewart demonstrated. His decision to select me as his senior enlisted leader at the Defense Intelligence Agency sparked considerable controversy. My position as master gunnery sergeant rather than sergeant major violated long-standing protocol. To civilians, this distinction might seem trivial, but in Marine Corps culture, it was akin to wearing combat boots to a state dinner. To simplify this, consider that the sergeant major takes on more of an administrative leadership role and the master gunnery sergeant an operational or subject matter expert role. Like all Marines, they are leaders as well, but rarely, in fact almost never, is one assigned outside of their rank. However, Lt. General Stewart was the new director of the Defense

Intelligence Agency, and he required a leader who understood the joint force and intelligence community while able to lead within a large agency. According to him, I was what he wanted. As you can imagine, that made things a little uncomfortable for me; however, I quickly got over that and took on my new role and responsibilities.

General Stewart used to joke that I had a "24-hour contract, renewable daily." He'd laugh when he said it, but we both knew he was putting his neck on the line for me. He didn't care about the old ways of doing things; he wanted what he called "the best athlete" for the position, and he thought that was me. His comment about the 24-hour contract was to reinforce the importance of validating one's credentials every day.

I learned something crucial from General Stewart that completely changed how I view leadership. It's not about rank or following tradition blindly. It's about genuinely caring for your people and having the guts to back that care with action, even when it makes others uncomfortable. Sometimes, traditions and the idea of how things have always been done need to be reviewed, and changes are in the best interest of the organization. In many ways, Lt. General Stewart was a man ahead of his time.

Now, I can practically hear some of you thinking, *Great, another touchy-feely leadership book.* Not exactly. What I'm talking about is understanding a simple truth: When people know you genuinely give a damn about them and their success, they'll run through walls for you. Not because they have to, but because they want to.

That's what this chapter is about—how real leadership starts with genuine care for your people, backed up by clear standards and accountability. It's a lesson that took me years to learn, and it's probably not what you'd expect from a Marine with three decades of service. But it works. You can tell your people you care, and they'll be grateful, but when you show someone you care, you have a teammate forever.

And look, I'll be honest; preparation and development matter a lot here. Whether you're talking about Michael Jordan getting cut from his high school basketball team or Tiger Woods picking up his first golf club, we all start somewhere. Nobody comes out fully formed as a leader. When you first take on any new role, there's going to be anxiety and nervousness. But here's how I've learned to look at it: Anxiety is just energy telling you that you care. And if you care, you care about the end result and the people you're serving.

Trust in Action

Let me share an experience that crystallizes what effective leadership looks like in action. For operational security reasons, I can't disclose all the details, but the lesson is clear enough.

During my time with General Stewart, we conducted partner engagements along the Russian border with NATO nations in Eastern Europe. Our mission included meetings with allied partners and embassy personnel, culminating in a crucial briefing with a U.S. ambassador scheduled for the following morning.

This is where traditional military protocol collided with real leadership. In our hierarchical structure, certain expectations are ironclad, chief among them being that someone of General Stewart's stature, the director of the Defense Intelligence Agency, doesn't delegate ambassador briefings. Most leaders in his position would deliver that briefing if they had to crawl there on hands and knees.

Military culture practically demands it.

But Stewart was different. He woke up that morning with one of those killer sore throats you get from aircraft air—any aircraft air; this wasn't some commercial flight but rather a military airlift because of his position and how close we were to Russia. So, what did he do? He sent me a text: "I'm not feeling well. You got it."

That's it. Three words. You. Got. It.

When I read those three words—*You. Got. It.*—a thousand things ran through my head. I didn't want to let him down. But it was bigger than that. I wanted to represent the Defense Intelligence Agency with excellence. I wanted to make the Marine Corps proud. I wanted to validate the trust he had placed in me, not just for that moment, but for all the moments that came before it. That message wasn't just about a briefing. It was a reminder that *he believed in me.*

And that belief did something to me. It challenged me to lead differently—to empower others the way he empowered me. I started looking for chances to give trust, not just demand it. That's the ripple effect of leadership love. It multiplies.

I almost had to read it twice. In my entire career, I'd never seen a general officer do something like that. They'd either reschedule or show up half-dead. But not Stewart.

So, there I was, putting on my coat and tie, about to brief our ambassador. Was I nervous? Hell yes. But here's the thing—Stewart hadn't brought me along as what we call a "traveling puppet" (you know, those folks who just sit there nodding and taking notes). He actually expected me to step up.

Let me tell you why this matters. In the military, especially in the Marine Corps, we're big on tradition. Like, *really* big. As I said earlier, Stewart caught a lot of flak just for picking me as his senior enlisted leader because I was a master gunnery sergeant, not a sergeant major.

That morning turned out to be one of the best days of my professional life. Not because I gave an amazing briefing—though I didn't screw it up, thankfully—but because someone I respected actually trusted me to deliver. It's tough for me to explain how much his confidence in me meant as I stood in front of someone of such seniority. He didn't ask me if I was ready or if I needed anything; he just told me I had it. Perhaps that's why he said we had a 24-hour contract; if my presentation with the ambassador didn't go well, my retirement ceremony would have been the next day. In this case, his trust in me showed his love and his belief in my leadership.

That's what I mean by leading with love. It's not about group hugs or lowering standards. It's about believing in your people enough to let them grow, even when it means breaking with tradition. And when someone shows that kind of trust in you? Man, you'll do anything to prove them right.

It reminds me of what preparation really means in leadership. You get 24 hours in a day, and that's it. But you can cheat those hours a bit by minimizing decisions ahead of time. It's like what we do with our daughters before school—everything goes in the van the night before. Backpacks, clothes laid out; everything is arranged and organized, ready for the day ahead. Not because we're control freaks, but because it creates space for what really matters: being present with our people when they need us.

The Hard Truth About Leadership Love

Even now, after 30-plus years in the Marine Corps, I still get weird looks when I talk about love in leadership. I get it; it's not exactly what you expect from a Marine.

The other day, I consulted with a certain company. They don't pay me exceptionally well, but I'll never leave them. Why? Because of the boss. This guy mentors me, molds me, gives me advice—heck, I could text him right now at dawn and he'd respond. He leads his organization with love.

Let me break it down clearly: Love isn't about being soft, it's about being committed. Love in leadership isn't softness, it's an investment in potential. And investment isn't always comfortable. It demands honest conversations, difficult calls, and believing in people before they believe in themselves. That's what real leaders do. They spot the spark in someone and commit to helping them develop it—sometimes with praise, often with pressure, always with purpose.

Love isn't easy. But it's effective. And it lasts.

Love is holding the line, giving honest feedback, and pushing people to rise to their potential. Love, in this context, is a choice to care deeply about someone's growth, even when it means having the hard conversations. It's discipline, backed by compassion. Expectation, grounded in trust.

—

Now, before you roll your eyes, let me explain what I mean by "love" in leadership. I'm not talking about group hugs and trust falls. I'm talking about accountability. If you don't hold people accountable for a standard, guess what? That standard's gone. Simple as that.

I learned this from working with some tough leaders. Take General Bob Neller, the former commandant of the Marine Corps—picture the crusty Marine warrior type. I once gave a fairly technical presentation on Cyberspace to a group of 50 DoD leaders attending a National Defense University class. After I had given this presentation, everyone told me how great I did. But I am always uncomfortable with group praise and reading my own headlines, so I approached my former commandant and asked what he thought.

He looked at me and said, "Do you really want to know?"

When a Marine general asks if you really want to know something, it's terrifying. But I said yes. He told me to meet him for breakfast the next morning. He started by saying I did a good job, then gave me two specific things to improve.

That's real leadership love right there. Not giving the easy compliments everyone else was giving me, but delivering the hard truth that helped me get better. If you want to be a leader one day, be both the person seeking to improve and the individual who can give honest feedback to the person striving to become better.

I see too many leaders who think they're showing love by constantly looking over people's shoulders. They micromanage everything because they "care so much about getting it right." But here's what really happens—their people stop taking initiative. They just wait to be told what to do.

There's a big difference between tough love and toxic leadership. Tough love is when you challenge your team to rise, not because you're controlling, but because you believe in them. It says, "I know you can do more, and I'll hold you to that." Toxic leadership, on the other hand, micromanages out of ego, control, or insecurity. It wears people down. If you're constantly correcting without connecting, you're not leading with love, you're just managing through fear.

Do you want to know what real leadership looks like? It's when your people succeed, and you're genuinely more excited than they are. When someone on my team gets promoted or their kid graduates college, to me, that's better than any personal win.

But here's the trap a lot of leaders fall into: they surround themselves with "yes men." People who tell them how amazing they are all day long. Sure, it feels good. But it's a guaranteed ticket to mediocrity.

I have a friend who's in charge of 11 fast-food restaurants in Ohio. Every time we talk, he asks for feedback. Not compliments, but real feedback. That's why he keeps growing while other businesses stay stuck.

Look, the military taught me something important: Comfort is the enemy of growth. If you want to be your best, you need people in your life who will tell you the truth. Not just critics; we've all got plenty of those. But people who actually want you to succeed and care enough to tell you when you're off track.

Do you know how I prep for public speaking now? I focus on three things. Just three. It could be about anything: NBA history, basketball, certain players, whatever. Just three key points. Then, depending on how long I have to speak, I may focus on three key things about each of those three topics. This is an easy trick that allows you to engage without notes instead of insulting your crowd by reading to them. Keeping it simple allows you to master the fundamentals. When you do something for the first time, you're probably not going to be your best. I've been playing golf for years, and I'm still not very good. But having that structure, that clarity, makes all the difference.

Fundamentals are built through reps and sets. Just like in the gym, you don't build strength from showing up once, you build it from repetition. Want to be a better communicator? Practice active listening every single day. Want to lead better meetings? Run hundreds of them and debrief yourself afterward. Want to get better at decision-making? Run through mental scenarios in your off-time. It's about deliberate practice. You don't rise to excellence by accident, you train for it.

I can't overstate the importance of having people in your life who'll give you real feedback. Not just the "good job" kind, but the kind that makes you better. Not just having them in your life but adjusting your mindset so you seek them out.

Growing up with early experiences of neglect and hardship gave me a perfect roadmap of everything I don't want to be as I turn 50. Sounds crazy, but I'm actually grateful for some of the tougher things I experienced growing up. Not because it was good—it wasn't—but because it showed me exactly what and who not to be. Sure, I want my daughters to experience some bumps in life, but without the bruises I had to take.

This reminds me of another tough lesson about growth and comfort. About a decade ago, I was dealing with killer back pain. The docs put me on intense pain meds, probably OxyContin, and I turned into a zombie. I couldn't wake up, I slept all the time, and felt like I was watching my own life happen.

Finally, I went to my boss, Brett, and told him I needed to retire. I couldn't live up to Marine Corps standards anymore; I couldn't even live up to my own standards. But instead of letting me quit,

I got introduced to a new fitness program created by U.S. Special Operations Command. I started powerlifting, of all things. I went from barely being able to move to competing in amateur power-lifting competitions. I even got my wife into it—she's still in the Pentagon Powerlifting Hall of Fame with her photo on the wall to this day.

Here's what all these stories have in common: Comfort is the enemy of growth. Whether you're in the military, running a business, or just trying to be better than you were yesterday, you need people who will challenge you to grow. When you truly care about your people, you don't just praise them, you push them to improve.

But don't forget this: Leadership love has to start with you. If you don't respect yourself—your health, your boundaries, your worth—you can't pour into others. I learned that the hard way, through injuries, exhaustion, and years of running on empty. You can't give what you don't have. Taking care of your own well-being isn't selfish, it's leadership prep. Because when you're at your best, you can give your best to your team.

And yes, sometimes that means having uncomfortable con-versations or hearing things you'd rather not hear. But that's what real leadership looks like. It's not about making people feel good all the time. It's about caring enough to help them become better. Something I always thought about as an active-duty Marine: You're not here to be liked (it's great when you are, but it's not a require-ment). You want to be able to look in the mirror and know you did everything you could to train others and prepare them for what may be the worst day of their lives. Sometimes they may not be happy with you, but when they return home from an operation or conflict, they'll know you loved them enough to train them well and that they were ready for whatever they had to face.

If you want to know whether you're leading with love, ask yourself these questions:

- Do I give honest feedback, even when it's uncomfortable?

- Do I care more about my people's long-term growth than my short-term popularity?

- Do my people know I have their back, even when I'm holding them accountable? Real love isn't about being liked. It's about being trusted when it matters most.

Growing Through Stress

A few years ago, I entered a powerlifting competition. One guy who competed against me was, without question, stronger than me. During warmups, he casually lifted weights I could barely manage at my maximum. When we got to the actual competition, he beat me by about 100 pounds in both the bench press and squat.

Then we got to the deadlift, and something happened—he tried to lift his weight and ripped his hamstring. Just like that, he was out. All I had to do was lift a couple hundred pounds more than my previous lifts and I would win. I did it; I put up a total of 1,325 pounds and took first place.

Here's the crazy part. Inside my head, I still felt like that skinny, geeky kid who joined the Marine Corps while barely making the minimum weight requirement. The one who couldn't get a date in high school, whom nobody talked to. Even after all those years of training, even after winning competitions, part of me was still that scrawny recruit.

But you know what? That's not necessarily a bad thing. You can't grow without introducing stress into your life. It's like my friend who owns the fast-food chains—he started as a teenager flipping burgers. Now he owns eleven locations. Every challenge he faced—market problems, COVID-19 throwing curveballs, dealing with poor management—helped him grow stronger.

From Nelson Mandela to the Korean War

Nelson Mandela exemplified this philosophy of leading with love. After spending 27 years in prison, enough time to build up a mountain of justified anger, he emerged to become South Africa's president. Rather than wielding an iron fist, he focused on reconciliation.

The power of his approach became clear when he invited one of his former white prison guards to his presidential inauguration. This wasn't merely a feel-good gesture, it was strategic leadership. Mandela understood that healing his nation mattered more than settling scores. That's real strength, not weakness.

Frances Perkins demonstrated similar courage through compassion. As the first woman appointed to a U.S. presidential cabinet, serving as FDR's Secretary of Labor, she transformed American workplace culture. In 1911, she witnessed the horrific Triangle Shirtwaist Factory fire, watching helplessly as workers, mostly young women, jumped to their deaths because the factory owners had locked the fire escapes.

She channeled that profound concern into action. Throughout her career, she fought for workplace safety, fair wages, and shorter workdays. When critics claimed she was "too soft" on business, she stood her ground. Her firsthand experience of the human cost of negligent leadership fueled her resolve.

General Matthew Ridgway's leadership in Korea particularly resonates with my military experience. In 1951, he assumed command of UN forces when morale had hit rock bottom. While traditional military doctrine might have suggested a tough, disciplinary approach, Ridgway dedicated his first weeks to visiting frontline troops, listening to their concerns, and ensuring they understood their mission's purpose.

The result? Those same demoralized troops began pushing the enemy back. Not because of threats or rank-pulling, but because Ridgway demonstrated that someone in command valued them as people, not just tactical assets.

These leaders embodied what General Stewart taught me: Authentic authority flows from genuine investment in people's success, not from position or rank. While some might dismiss this approach as soft, I've witnessed it achieve results that no amount of authoritarian leadership could match.

These leaders understood exactly what General Stewart taught me: Real authority doesn't come from your rank or position. It comes from genuine investment in your people's success. Some folks might call this approach soft. But I've seen it produce results that no amount of tough-guy leadership could achieve.

Retired Army Four-Star General Paul Nakasone is also the former director of the NSA and a mentor of mine; I had the great privilege of serving with him and learned about leadership through his acts and deeds. He often texts or calls, and regardless of the main point, he asks how my wife Malerie and the girls are doing. Now, he's doing great things—he's on the board for OpenAI, and he's the founding director of the Institute of National Security at Vanderbilt University—but he still takes time to care about people as individuals. That's why when he asked me to come speak at Vanderbilt about leadership, I didn't even ask about payment or logistics. I just said yes, because I trust him completely and because I know about the quality of talent he invites and the expectation of excellence in everything he does.

That kind of leadership, where people will follow you not because they have to, but because they want to, happens when you genuinely invest in people's growth and success. And sometimes that means putting them under stress, like adding weight to a barbell. It's not about breaking them. It's about making them stronger.

I remember one moment, late in my career, when a junior Marine came back from a deployment and handed me a challenge coin. I didn't recognize him at first. He said, "You probably don't remember, but years ago you chewed me out for not being ready. You held me to a standard no one else had. At the time, I was angry. But that moment changed everything for me. I stayed in because of it." That's when it hit me—he didn't come back to thank me because I was nice. He came back because he knew I cared.

When I first joined the Corps, if you'd told me I'd be talking about love and leadership, I would've thought you were crazy. But preparation for tomorrow begins tonight; that's something else I've learned. Whether you're getting ready for a presentation, a difficult conversation, or just the next day of leading your team, taking time to think through how you'll show up for your people makes all the difference.

And it's not just about the big moments. It's about the small daily practices that build trust. When my daughters say thank you, I tell them to look me in the eye when they say it. Not to be strict, but because it builds confidence. Because someday, they'll need to look their own teams in the eye and lead them.

Here's how you know the difference:

Leading with Love

Builds trust
Gives feedback to help you grow
Delegates with belief
Cares about long-term development

Leading with Fear

Breeds silence
Criticizes to stay in control
Micromanages out of insecurity
Obsesses over short-term perfection

Here's something I do with my family to drive home what I mean about making connections. Every time we go out to dinner, I tell my four and five-year-old daughters that they'll earn a dollar if they can remember our server's first name by the end of the meal. It's amazing to watch them pay attention and listen carefully when the server introduces themselves.

And you know what? It's not really about the dollar. I learned from Dale Carnegie's book, *How to Win Friends and Influence People,* that the most powerful thing you can do is call someone by their name. When my girls get it right and use that server's name at the end of the meal, they're not just earning a buck. They're learning how to make real connections with people. How to show someone they matter.

Let me wrap this up with something important: Leadership is a position we all lease; we don't own it forever. If you don't validate your credentials every single day, people will do things just because you're in a position of authority. They'll follow orders because they have to.

But when you lead with love—real love, the kind backed by accountability and trust—people do things because they want to. That's when you achieve a culture that's operating at its best.

Leadership isn't about your rank or title. It's not about being the boss. It's about creating an environment where people feel valued, where they're held to high standards, and where they know, *really* know, that you care about their success.

Simple concept. Hard to execute. But it's worth every ounce of effort it takes.

That's why I loved General Stewart's "24-hour contract." It wasn't just about proving your worth; it was about showing your people that *they matter enough to be challenged.* It was daily trust, daily accountability, and daily belief. That's love in action.

Love shows up in leadership when:

- You ask how someone's doing—and wait for the answer.
- You push someone to step up because you believe they can.
- You remember someone's kid's name and ask about their graduation.
- You say "no" to protect their time.
- You give the hard feedback no one else will.

Ask yourself this tonight: Who needs to know I believe in them? And what am I going to do tomorrow to show them?

As Brené Brown puts it, "Clear is kind. Unclear is unkind." That's what love looks like in leadership—being honest, even when it's hard. It's clarity that helps people grow. It's truth, delivered with care.

CHAPTER TAKEAWAYS:

- Real leadership power comes from trust, not rank. As General Stewart showed me, when you trust your people enough to let them step up, they'll exceed your expectations every time.

- When you hold people accountable, you're showing them you care. The moment you stop maintaining standards is the moment you stop helping your people grow.

- Watch out for "yes men." Surround yourself with people who care enough to tell you the hard truths, like General Neller did for me. Comfort is the enemy of growth.

- You must earn trust daily. Just like I tell my daughters about remembering the server's name, it's the small actions, done consistently, that build real connections.

- Leadership isn't about making people feel good, it's about making them better. As in powerlifting, you need to introduce stress to create growth. But there's a difference between challenging people and breaking them.

*"We are what we repeatedly do.
Excellence, then, is not an act, but a habit."
— Aristotle*

— 3 —

MINDSET MASTERY:
TURNING INTENTIONS INTO IMPACT

"Sir, the Secretary of the Navy can't make it. Can you do the keynote?"

Thousands of people. No preparation. Three hours' notice. I was sitting at lunch during the Space Symposium with my boss, a Four-Star General, when those words hit me like a thunderbolt. The staff member who'd rushed to our table was waiting for an answer, sweat beading on his forehead. In my heart, I wanted to say, "Hell yes!" But in the military, you don't just step in for the Secretary of the Navy without proper clearance. My mind was already racing through what I'd say to that massive audience, even as I waited for my boss's approval.

Here's what they don't teach you in leadership courses: Sometimes, the biggest moments of your career arrive disguised as impossible challenges. It's not about being ready. It's about staying ready.

There I was, completely unprepared, being asked to speak to thousands of people in just a few hours. Once my boss, U.S. Army General James Dickinson, gave the green light, I had a choice to make: panic about my lack of preparation or trust in my ability to deliver.

I chose to visualize excellence. Instead of fixating on all the ways I could fail, I saw myself succeeding. I pictured people clapping, smiling, engaged. I ran through the entire event in my mind before I ever stepped on that stage.

The feedback afterward? A recently retired Four-Star General and well-known leader in the space community approached me and said, "In the history of this event, that was the best presentation we've ever had."

You could say that made my day.

But this isn't a story about natural talent or even experience. It's about the power of the mind to shape reality. About how our thoughts, when properly focused and channeled, can transform into decisive action. Most importantly, it's about the critical mental work that has to happen "Left of Leadership" before you ever step into the spotlight.

That's what this chapter is really about. Mental mastery is Left of Leadership. The way you think before the pressure hits—that's what shapes your impact when it does. Before you step on the stage, before you lead the team, before you wear the title, you train your mindset. In silence. In solitude. In the reps no one sees.

In this chapter, we'll explore how to harness the power of your mind to become a more effective leader. We'll discuss mental toughness and resilience, the gift of stress, and how habits of thought lead to habits of action. Most importantly, we'll talk about how to overcome the biggest obstacle any leader faces: the limitations we place on ourselves.

Because here's the truth: Before you can lead others, you have to master your own mind. The ceiling you place on yourself will become the ceiling for your entire team. Let's break through those limitations together.

The Mental Edge

Let's talk about what happens in your mind when facing a challenge. During that Space Symposium presentation, I wasn't just winging it, I was leveraging years of mental preparation. It's about developing what I call "left of the moment" thinking—the mental work that happens before you're in the spotlight.

Here's what most people don't understand about mental preparation: it's not just positive thinking. It's about building mental pathways for success through deliberate practice. When I train teams now, I start by asking them to walk me through their thought process before any major challenge. Most of them focus on what could go wrong. That's natural, but it's not productive. Instead, I focus on what could go right. When I practice or rehearse, I don't just run through my material, I visualize excellence. I picture the crowd clapping. I hear someone saying, "That was exactly what we needed." I imagine what success feels like before I ever walk on stage. That way, when it actually happens, I'm ready for it. I can receive it without letting it go to my head, because in my mind, I've already been there.

That's the difference between being surprised by success and being prepared for it.

And here's the real power in that—when you've already seen it in your mind, you don't freeze or fumble when it happens in real life. You step into the moment with quiet confidence, not ego. You don't need to celebrate like it's the first time, because in your mind, it's not. That's what separates professionals from performers. The pros have rehearsed the win a thousand times before the crowd ever shows up.

—

But visualizing success doesn't mean ignoring reality. I also teach them to build mental contingency plans, like a chess player who's always thinking several moves ahead. It's not enough to believe you'll win; you've got to mentally rehearse how you'll respond when things don't go according to plan. This isn't about removing uncertainty. It's about preparing your mind to stay steady when it shows up.

Let me give you an example from my time at Space Command. When we were developing our operations plans, we didn't just plan for the ideal scenario. We had to think through every possible way things could go sideways. What if communications were disrupted? What if we lost satellite capability? What if our allies couldn't support us? By mentally walking through these scenarios ahead of time, we built confidence in our ability to handle whatever came our way.

This kind of mental preparation creates what psychologists call "response readiness." When you've mentally rehearsed different scenarios, your brain doesn't freeze when challenges arise; it simply executes what you've already practiced. It's the difference between reacting and responding.

The key is understanding that mental toughness isn't about never feeling fear or doubt—it's about having practiced responses to those feelings. As the Greek poet Archilochus put it, "We don't rise to the level of our expectations, we fall to the level of our training." Just like building physical muscle memory, mental resilience comes from repetition and preparation. Every time you face a challenge and work through it mentally before it happens, you're strengthening those neural pathways, ensuring that when the moment comes, you don't have to rely on sheer willpower but can trust in the training you've put in.

This is why the most effective leaders aren't just the ones with the most experience. They are the ones who've done the most thorough mental preparation. They've trained their minds to see opportunities where others see obstacles, and to find solutions where others see problems.

Your mind is like a pilot's checklist. You don't wait until you're in an emergency to figure out what to do. You run through the scenarios ahead of time, prepare your responses, and trust your training when the moment comes. That's how you transform thoughts into effective action.

When Thoughts Become Actions

Habits of thought lead to habits of action. It sounds simple, but I've seen this principle make or break careers, relationships, and entire organizations. Think about the world we live in right now: 24/7 news telling us everything's on fire, social media feeding us endless negativity, constant crisis mode. If you let those thought patterns dominate your mind, guess what kind of actions follow?

Let me get practical for a minute. Recently, I made a decision to stop drinking for 100 days. Not because I had a serious problem; I could handle my liquor just fine, maybe too well. After 31 years in the Marine Corps, I was used to having structure and discipline imposed from outside. But in retirement, working remotely, running my own company, I found myself having a cocktail at noon, then another at one, and this was becoming a daily pattern.

Here's the thing. I didn't like who I was becoming, not because of any dramatic incidents but because I was letting my standards slip. I was losing that discipline that had defined my career. So, I decided to stop. Not forever necessarily, but for now and probably until my 50th birthday. It wasn't about the drinking itself, it was about regaining control of my habits.

Winners surround themselves with winners. It's another simple principle with profound implications. Instead of consuming endless negative news, I seek out wisdom. I listen to powerful TED talks. I read good books. These habits of thought lead to habits of positive action—waking up early, working out, investing in personal growth.

But here's the critical part—you can't just be a dreamer. You have to be a doer. I've learned there are two competing ways to measure success: measurement of performance versus measurement of effectiveness. Performance means you might have done something ten times. Effective means you actually achieved the desired outcome.

Prior to the Japanese attack on Pearl Harbor, a certain naval officer, Lieutenant Commander Edwin T. Layton, was an attaché in Japan. He conveyed to American military leadership that Japan intended to invade America. He performed his duty by reporting what he knew. But he wasn't effective. He wasn't compelling enough in his delivery, in his urgency. The message didn't land. We all know what happened at Pearl Harbor.

Similarly, Billy Mitchell, considered the godfather of the Air Force, outlined exactly how an air attack on Pearl Harbor might happen. The leadership at the time dismissed him, saying aircraft were just "flying kites." They couldn't see the threat because he couldn't make them see it.

The lesson here? Your thoughts and knowledge aren't enough; you have to be able to transform them into effective action. This is where it's important to emphasize my point about measurements of effectiveness over measurements of performance. It's not enough to simply take action or repeat a task countless times; you have to be effective, or it doesn't matter. A leader who speaks or acts without impact might as well have done nothing at all.

Here's the difference: You can run ten meetings and still not move the mission. That's performance. But if one conversation shifts strategy, creates alignment, or inspires action? That's effectiveness. Leaders get measured by the outcomes they create, not just the activity they complete.

There's an old Japanese proverb I love: "Vision without action is a daydream. Action without vision is a nightmare." You need both. You need to align your words with action, walk the talk, and lead by example. When you tell your team they need to achieve 10% growth next month, you'd better have visualized it and believed it first. Because if you don't, they'll smell out your doubt and fear.

This is why we must be so careful about our thought patterns.

If you're constantly consuming negative input, constantly doubting yourself, constantly focusing on what could go wrong, those thoughts will manifest in your actions. Your team will pick up on it. They'll reflect it back.

Instead, surround yourself with wise men and women. Find people who have achieved success in the way you want to. Look for kind people, genuine people who support each other's success. This isn't just positive thinking, it's creating an environment that nurtures positive action.

Think about putting your gym bag in your car the night before. Getting your kids' stuff ready for school the next day. These small habits of preparation aren't just about efficiency, they're about building a pattern of positive action that starts with positive thought. It also keeps you from being in a rush, enabling you to think clearly and make smart decisions.

The discipline of daily action is what separates average from great. It's not about doing something once and declaring victory. It's about consistent, repeated effort over time. As Robert Collier said, "Success is the sum of small efforts, repeated day in and day out."

Remember this: What you think about consistently becomes what you do consistently. And what you do consistently becomes who you are. Because today, you are creating the person you will become three years from now. Choose your thoughts carefully; they're the seeds of your actions.

Breaking Through Self-Imposed Limits

Before you can lead others, you must conquer the toughest opponent you'll ever face: self-doubt. In the military, we often create artificial ceilings for ourselves. We have an outdated Napoleonic rank structure: this is what this rank does, these are your boundaries, don't step outside these lines. Sound familiar? Even if you're not in the military, I bet you've run into similar invisible barriers in your own career.

I have battled with imposter syndrome. In 2012, I'd been wearing the rank of Master Gunnery Sergeant E9, our highest enlisted rank, for about two years. I was stationed at Camp Lejeune as the Intel chief for Marine Corps Forces Special Operations Command. They sent me to give a presentation at Special Operations Command headquarters, in Tampa, Florida, speaking to a room full of Navy SEALs, Marine Special Ops Raiders, and Green Berets.

Here's where it gets embarrassing. On my way to the conference, I actually stopped at a store looking for a "touch of gray" hair color. I was surrounded by weathered, seasoned operators, and I thought they'd see right through me if I didn't look older. How ridiculous is that? I was focusing on symbolism over substance, worrying about how I looked instead of what I knew.

The next day, I gave my presentation about our Multi-Discipline Intelligence Operators Course. Do you know what happened? Those same operators I was so intimidated by came up afterward to congratulate me. They didn't care how old I looked or how much gray was in my hair. They cared about competence.

This is a crucial lesson about leadership: The greatest obstacles we face are almost always internal. The ceiling you place on yourself becomes the ceiling for your entire team. If you tell your team they need to achieve 10% growth next month, but you don't truly believe it's possible, they'll sense that doubt. They'll smell your fear.

Think about it—how many times have you talked yourself out of opportunity because you didn't think you were ready? How many times have you waited for permission instead of taking the initiative? How many times have you let self-doubt win?

In the military, we have an outdated mindset that certain ranks can't do certain things. But great leaders understand that the most significant barriers they face aren't in their job description, they're in their own mind. That's why I tell people that before you can lead others effectively, you must conquer these internal battles.

Here's what I've learned: Self-doubt is natural. Even today, with all my experience, I still battle it. When I'm preparing to write this book or give a speech, those old questions creep in. Am I qualified enough? Do I have enough to say? Will people find value in this? I try to remember what the Jedi Master Yoda in *Star Wars* said: *"Do or do not, there is no try."*

But I've learned to recognize those thoughts for what they are—just thoughts. They're not facts. They're not limitations. They're just patterns of thinking that we can choose to accept or challenge.

Remember that Space Symposium story I opened with? If I had let self-doubt win in that moment, if I had focused on all the reasons I wasn't prepared or qualified enough to step in for the Secretary of the Navy, I would have missed an incredible opportunity. Instead, I chose to focus on what I could bring to that moment and the thousands in attendance gave me a standing ovation when it was over.

The key is to understand that leadership isn't about never having doubts but about not letting those doubts control your actions. It's about recognizing when that little voice in your head is protecting you from genuine danger versus when it's just trying to keep you safely in your comfort zone.

Because growth never happens in your comfort zone. Just like building muscle requires stress on your body, building leadership requires stress on your capabilities. You have to be willing to step into situations that make you uncomfortable, to take on challenges that seem just a little bit beyond your current abilities.

That's how you expand your limits. That's how you grow. That's how you lead.

That's the edge where transformation lives—just past your comfort zone, where fear and growth collide. Most people retreat at that threshold. Leaders press forward. They recognize the discomfort not as a threat, but as a signal that they're on the verge of becoming someone new.

The Power of Belief

The quote of Henry Ford's I chose to open this chapter with bears repeating: *"Whether you think you can or you think you can't, you are right."* After thirty years of leadership experience, I can tell you this isn't just a clever quote, it's a fundamental truth about success. Your belief drives action, and your action determines results.

Let me put this in practical terms. When I'm helping organizations develop leaders, I often ask them a simple question: What does success look like to you next month? Next year? Five years from now? The answers tell me a lot, not just about their goals but about their beliefs about what's possible.

Here's a trick I've learned: I tell leaders they need to be able to explain their plan, their vision, to a group of five-year-olds. This isn't about dumbing things down, it's about forcing clarity, getting rid of the garbage and acronyms that often mask a lack of real conviction. Because if you can't explain where you're going in simple terms, chances are you don't really believe in it yourself.

This ties back to what Ford understood: Your beliefs shape your reality. When I work with teams now, I see this play out all the time. Leaders who believe in their vision, who have truly internalized it, communicate differently. They inspire differently. They lead differently than those who are just going through the motions.

Think about the four-minute mile. For years, people believed it was impossible for a human being to run a mile in under four minutes. It was a physical barrier, they said. It couldn't be done. Then Roger Bannister did it in 1954. Within just a year, several other runners had done it too. What changed? Not human physiology. What changed was what people believed was possible.

The same principle applies to leadership. Your belief in what's possible—for yourself, your team, your organization—sets the ceiling for what you can achieve. This isn't positive thinking nonsense. This is about the direct connection between what you believe and what you're willing to attempt.

I see leaders limit themselves and their teams all the time with phrases like "That's just how we've always done it" or "That's not how things work here." These aren't just statements. They're beliefs that become self-fulfilling prophecies.

This is why it's so crucial that your leadership is driven by your morals, values, character, and sense of purpose. When you know your "why," when you're clear about your purpose, like Viktor Frankl talks about in his book, *Man's Search for Meaning*, your belief has a foundation. It's not just wishful thinking, it's conviction based on something real.

But remember—belief without action is just daydreaming. Success isn't about doing something once or just believing you can do it. It's about consistent, repeated action driven by unshakeable belief. It's about disciplining yourself to take daily action; that's what separates average from great.

The power of belief extends beyond individual achievement. When you truly believe in your vision, when you've internalized it completely, it shows in everything you do. Your team doesn't just hear what you're saying, they feel your conviction. They sense your certainty. And that's when the magic happens. That's when they start believing too.

As Ford knew, and as I've seen countless times in my career, what you believe about yourself, your team, and what's possible, becomes the foundation for everything that follows. Choose those beliefs carefully. Make them big enough to inspire but specific enough to act on. Then back them up with consistent action.

Vague goals create vague effort. But when your belief is crystal clear—when you can articulate it, visualize it, and feel it in your gut—it activates action. It gives your team something to aim at, not just something to hope for.

Because in the end, Henry Ford was right—whether you think you can or think you can't, you're probably right. The choice is yours.

Mental Fortitude in the Face of Fire

Consider Admiral James Stockdale, one of the most powerful examples of mental discipline in military history. Shot down over North

Vietnam in 1965, he spent seven and a half years as a prisoner of war.[1] What many people don't know is that before his capture, Stockdale had immersed himself in the writings of ancient Stoic philosophers, particularly Epictetus. This mental preparation, something he did with no knowledge of what was coming, would prove crucial to his survival and leadership.[2]

During his imprisonment at the infamous "Hanoi Hilton," Stockdale faced routine torture, isolation, and brutal conditions. But he didn't just survive. He led. He developed an elaborate communication system among prisoners, maintained a command presence even in isolation, and helped other POWs resist their captors.[3] When asked later how he managed this, Stockdale explained that his philosophical training had taught him to focus on what he could control—his responses, his attitude, his mental state—rather than what he couldn't.[4]

Stockdale had trained his mind to turn inward for strength when external circumstances offered none. This wasn't just positive thinking; it was disciplined mental preparation put into decisive action under the most challenging conditions imaginable.

What's particularly relevant for us is how Stockdale approached each day. He never let himself be optimistic about quick rescue or release. Instead, he focused on maintaining absolute faith that he would eventually prevail while confronting the brutal facts of his current reality. This balance, between unshakeable faith and clear-eyed realism, is exactly what we need as leaders.[5] It's about preparing your mind not just for success, but for the difficult journey success requires.

Visualizing the Impossible

The power of transforming thoughts into action is perhaps best illustrated by Florence Nightingale's revolutionary approach to battlefield medicine. When she arrived at the British military hospital in Scutari during the Crimean War in 1854, she encountered conditions that most people would have deemed hopeless. But Nightingale didn't just see what was, she envisioned what could be.[6]

Unlike her predecessors, Nightingale believed that deaths in military hospitals weren't inevitable, they were preventable. This radical shift in thinking led her to approach the problem in an entirely new way. Rather than accepting the conventional wisdom that high mortality rates were normal in wartime, she began meticulously collecting and analyzing data about why soldiers were dying.[7]

That's what leaders do. They don't just absorb the problem, they reframe it. They change how others see it. Florence didn't just fight disease, she fought indifference, inertia, and outdated assumptions. She didn't wait for permission. She saw a future others didn't, and then made it visible.

What made Nightingale's approach truly revolutionary was how she transformed complex statistical data into visual representations that anyone could understand. She developed what she called "coxcombs"—circular diagrams that clearly showed preventable deaths far outnumbered deaths from battle wounds.[8] This wasn't just data collection; it was a fundamental reimagining of how to present information to create change. When military officials said they couldn't "see" the problem, she literally showed them.[9]

Through her innovative use of statistics and visualization, Nightingale proved that poor sanitation was killing more soldiers than enemy weapons. Her data showed that for every soldier who died from battle wounds, seven were dying from preventable diseases.[10] This mental reframing—from accepting deaths as inevitable to seeing them as preventable—led to systematic changes that revolutionized military medicine and saved countless lives.[11]

Looking Ahead: Fueling the Fire

As we move into Chapter 4, we'll explore why drive outpaces grit in leadership success. You've learned how to master your mind and transform thoughts into action. Now we'll examine what fuels sustained leadership performance over the long haul.

The mental toughness and habits we've discussed in this chapter aren't just about personal achievement, they're the foundation for inspiring and motivating others. Because here's the truth: A leader's mindset is contagious. Your team will never believe in possibilities you don't believe in yourself. They'll never push harder than you're willing to push. They'll never reach higher than you're willing to reach.

Your team reflects your mindset more than your message. They respond to your energy, your belief, and your standards. If you're sharp, they sharpen. If you're complacent, they coast. Leadership is less about what you say and more about who you are when no one's watching.

Get ready to discover why some leaders seem to have an inexhaustible drive while others burn out. We'll explore how to kindle the kind of internal fire that not only sustains your own leadership journey but ignites passion in others.

The work you've done on mastering your mind sets the stage for what comes next. Because once you understand how to transform your own thoughts into action, you're ready to learn how to fuel that same transformation in others. That's when leadership becomes not just about what you can do, but about what you can inspire others to become.

Begin Your Mental Preparation Practice

Start by establishing a daily visualization routine. Before any significant event or challenge, take time to see yourself succeeding. Make it specific and detailed—if you're preparing for a presentation, visualize the room, the audience's engagement, the questions you might receive. Each evening, prepare mentally for the next day's challenges. Write down what worked and what didn't in your preparation approach. Over time, you'll develop a mental preparation system that works uniquely for you. I like to call this the "Visualizing the Championship Trophy" moment. See yourself winning and succeeding, your team exceeding their goals, and "getting the trophy" at the awards ceremony. Before I do it, I've already won because I've visualized it.

Harness Productive Stress

Take an honest inventory of areas where you need growth. Instead of avoiding stress, start deliberately seeking challenges that push you just slightly beyond your current capabilities. This might mean volunteering for that project nobody wants or taking on a responsibility that makes you slightly uncomfortable. Keep a journal of how you respond to these stressful situations and what you learn from them. Remember, the goal isn't to overwhelm yourself but to create the kind of productive stress that leads to growth.

Transform Your Thought Patterns

Take a hard look at what's feeding your mind each day. What media are you consuming? Who are you spending time with? What conversations dominate your day? Start consciously curating these inputs. When you catch yourself in negative thought patterns, practice redirecting them toward productive alternatives. This isn't about forced positivity, it's about choosing thoughts that lead to constructive action.

Push Past Your Perceived Limits

Take time to write down what you believe your limitations are, then question each one. Where did this belief come from? What evidence supports it? What would be possible if this limitation didn't exist? Choose one goal that seems just beyond possible, something that excites and scares you in equal measure. Then find someone who has already achieved something similar. Their success is evidence that your "impossible" might just be possible after all.

Develop Leadership Habits

Start with your daily routines. Establish a morning practice that sets you up for success and an evening routine that prepares you for tomorrow. Focus on small, consistent actions rather than dramatic changes. Maybe it's reading for 30 minutes each morning or spending time planning each evening. Whatever habits you choose, remember that consistency matters more than intensity. Small actions, repeated daily, create lasting change.

These aren't just tasks to check off a list. They're practices to be developed over time. Start where you are, be patient with your progress, and keep pushing forward. The mental strength you build today becomes the leadership capability you rely on tomorrow.

From Mindset to Movement

Throughout this chapter, we've explored how mental mastery translates into leadership effectiveness. From visualizing success at the Space Symposium to understanding the gift of stress, from breaking through self-imposed limits to harnessing the power of belief—these aren't just concepts. They're tools that, when properly applied, transform potential into performance.

Leadership starts in your mind long before it shows in your actions. Your thoughts become your habits, your habits become your character, and your character becomes your legacy as a leader. Choose those thoughts carefully, challenge your limitations regularly, and never underestimate the power of a well-prepared mind. Because to be an effective leader, it's not just about communication but demonstration. In other words, don't just talk the talk, walk the walk.

If you're walking it, others will follow. Leadership by example isn't a strategy, it's a standard. You can't ask for discipline, vision, or drive from others if they don't see it in you first. That's why I always say, before you lead others, lead yourself—daily, consistently, and with purpose.

The path from thought to action isn't always straight or simple. But with consistent practice, deliberate preparation, and unwavering belief, you can build the mental foundation necessary for effective leadership.

This is the frontline of leadership: the battle that begins in your own mind. If you want to lead others, start by mastering yourself.

The mindset work? The daily reps? The discipline no one sees?

That's Left of Leadership.

And if you build it right, no spotlight will ever shake you.

CHAPTER TAKEAWAYS:

- Mental preparation is as crucial as physical preparation for leadership success.
- Stress, when properly understood and utilized, becomes a tool for growth.
- Your habits of thought directly influence your habits of action.
- The biggest limitations leaders face are usually self-imposed.
- Belief backed by consistent action creates transformational results.

"Be a yardstick of quality.
Some people aren't used to an environment
where excellence is expected."
— Steve Jobs

— 4 —

MASTERING THE FUNDAMENTALS: THE ART OF BEING A WELL-ROUNDED LEADER

I've seen Marines spend eight hours rehearsing a ten-minute drill. Not because they had to, but because they knew lives could depend on it. Mastery doesn't start with glory. It starts in the grind.

Success leaves clues if you know where to look. Take my friend Josh, whom we discussed earlier in the book and who owns the fast food restaurants in Ohio. Most people see the end result—the successful business owner with multiple locations, a beautiful home, and nice vacations. What they don't see is where his journey really began: behind the grill, flipping burgers in high school.

"I had to master those basics and fundamentals first," he told me, "before I could even think about owning the business." Not everyone has to start that way, but that early experience gave Josh something invaluable—empathy. When COVID-19 threw curveballs at his business, when market challenges hit, and when he dealt with poor management, he had a foundation to draw from. He'd experienced every level of the operation, understood every role, felt every frustration. He'd done the work Left of Leadership.

That's what most people miss. The shine of success is built in the shadows—when no one's watching, when the paycheck is small, when the title hasn't come yet. But that's where character and capability are forged. The real work of leadership starts long before you ever get the position.

This is where the military does something right that many organizations miss: no one comes in at the top. In the Marine Corps, I don't care who you are or what your eventual role might be, everyone starts with the basics. We have the longest boot camp of any service branch, focused entirely on mastering fundamentals. Then we add infantry training and more fundamentals. Only after that foundation is solid do we let people specialize.

I learned this lesson myself during my time serving with General Stewart at the Defense Intelligence Agency, when we were traveling to South Florida where he was supposed to address a crowd of about 150 people. Just before the event, he looked at me and said, "You go first." No warning, no prep time. Just an expectation that I'd be ready.

Leadership at the highest levels will often throw you curveballs like that. The only way to handle them is to have such a solid grasp of the fundamentals that you can perform under any circumstances. Great leaders understand that their success is built on the strong foundation of these fundamental skills—the basics done extraordinarily well.

I've seen young Marines execute life-saving decisions under fire, not because they were experienced, but because they'd rehearsed every step until it was instinct. That's the power of the basics. They hold up when everything else breaks down.

"Amateurs train until they get it right. Professionals train until they cannot get it wrong." – José N. Harri, Army Special Forces Medical Sergeant & PhD.

I'm not talking about just technical skills here. I'm talking about the full spectrum of capabilities that make a well-rounded leader: decision-making, problem-solving, communication in all its forms, and perhaps most importantly, the ability to listen. These aren't advanced techniques, they're fundamentals. But like any fundamental skill, they must be practiced until they become second nature.

The problem is that too many aspiring leaders want to skip this part. They want to jump straight to strategy and vision without mastering the basics of human interaction. They want to run before they can walk. But in my experience, that's a recipe for failure.

In this chapter, we're going to explore what it means to master the fundamentals of leadership. We'll talk about why being well-rounded isn't just a nice-to-have but is essential. And we'll look at how to develop these skills systematically, deliberately, and effectively.

Because the basics aren't basic. They're the foundation on which everything else is built. And like any foundation, if they're weak, everything above them eventually crumbles.

Mastering the fundamentals isn't the prelude to leadership, it *is* leadership.

Once the foundation is strong, what fuels your next level isn't more knowledge, it's more drive.

Let's dive in.

The Art of Decision-Making

At some point in your leadership journey, you've got to take all the information you've received, your education, and your experience and use it as wisdom to make a decision. That's what leaders do. We don't just collect information or hold meetings. We decide.

I learned this lesson early in my career: The hardest problems get brought to leaders because that's why we're in charge. If the problems were easy, they would have been solved at a lower level. Your job as a leader isn't to complain about the difficulty, it's to make the call and own the outcome.

Here's what I tell my teams: You won't always get it right, but if you apply the basics and fundamentals to making that decision, you'll be able to sleep well at night knowing you tried to do what was best. That's not just feel-good advice, it's practical wisdom. Because the reality is that you'll face problems that don't have perfect solutions. You'll deal with situations that have no precedent in your experience.

And when you sleep well, you lead well. Because a leader who's constantly second-guessing themselves becomes hesitant, and hesitant leadership erodes trust. People don't follow perfect leaders; they follow decisive ones who are willing to learn, own mistakes, and keep moving forward.

Take the global pandemic as an example. Nobody had a playbook for that. But if you look back through history, you can find similar challenges that leaders had to navigate. The specifics might be different, but the fundamentals of crisis leadership remain remarkably consistent. Good leaders understand this. They know how to look back through history—at their own experiences or the country's or the world's—to find patterns and principles they can apply to current challenges.

I saw this play out at Space Command when we were developing our operations plan. We were dealing with incredibly complex, technical issues about space assets and capabilities. But at its core, the challenge wasn't technical. It was human. How do you communicate complex ideas clearly? How do you build consensus across different branches of service? How do you make decisions with incomplete information?

The fundamentals of good decision-making haven't changed much since Napoleon's time. Yes, the technology is different. Yes, the speed of information has increased exponentially. But the basic principles of gathering information, analyzing options, making a decision, and owning the outcome remain constant.

That's why when I'm faced with a tough decision, I focus on these fundamentals:

1. Get the best information available, but don't wait for perfect information

2. Consider the impact on all stakeholders

3. Make the call

4. Communicate effectively

5. Own the outcome

6. Learn from the results

Notice what's not on that list? Waiting for consensus. Finding someone else to blame if things go wrong. Making excuses for delayed decisions. Those aren't options for real leaders.

Think about the problems facing your organization right now. I guarantee the toughest ones aren't technical, they're human. They involve competing priorities, limited resources, and conflicting personalities. That's why mastering the fundamentals of decision-making is so crucial. Because when the pressure is on and the stakes are high, you won't have time to flip through a leadership manual. You'll fall back on your foundational skills and habits.

When COVID-19 hit, Josh had to make tough decisions daily—about staffing, about safety protocols, about staying open or closing locations. The fact that he'd started at the bottom, understanding every aspect of the business, gave him the foundation to make those calls. He might not have always been right, but he could sleep at night knowing his decisions were grounded in a solid understanding of the fundamentals.

That's what real leadership looks like: not having all the answers but having the courage to make decisions anyway. Not being perfect but being principled in your approach. Not avoiding tough calls but owning them completely.

It's the same on the battlefield, in business, or at the dinner table with your family. People don't expect perfection, they expect presence. When you show up consistently and make decisions from a place of principle, people will follow.

Because at the end of the day, that's what you're there for. To solve problems. To make decisions. To lead.

The Power of Communication

Let me teach you something that took me years to understand: When you're communicating as a leader, only 7% of what people connect with are your actual words. I know—it seems impossible, right? We spend so much time practicing our words, perfecting our presentations, and crafting our messages. But here's the breakdown that changed how I think about communication:

- 7% is your words
- 38% is your tonality and eye contact
- 55% is your body language

They call it the 7-38-55 rule, and understanding it transformed my approach to leadership communication. Think about that for a minute. Over 90% of your message comes from how you say something, not what you say.

I learned this lesson the hard way. When I was at United States Cyber Command and Space Command, I would often hear leaders talk to those who weren't in the technical field as if they were "in the club." They'd use all the right terminology, have all the right information, but completely lose their audience. I'd watch people mentally check out, nodding off during crucial briefings.

You've probably experienced this as a speaker too. You're standing there, trying to get your point across, and you can feel the energy draining from the room. That's what happens when we focus on the 7% and ignore the 93%.

The same message delivered with a confident posture and engaged eye contact lands completely differently than one mumbled into a laptop.

Here's what I do differently now: I focus first on body language and tonality. If you come out hunched over with your arms crossed, it doesn't matter how brilliant your words are because people will sense that closed-off energy and respond in kind. Stand up straight, pull your shoulders back, and make eye contact. Here's a personal trick: I consciously remind myself to smile, especially because I can be a very serious person by nature.

For example, yesterday, I worked with a CEO who was preparing to moderate a panel. She had great questions prepared, but she kept looking down at her notes while asking them, then looking down again to thank the speakers. I told her, "When you ask the question, look them in the eye. When you thank them, look them in the eye." When a moderator is looking down at their notes, it sends a subtle message: *We need to move on to the next question.* Your answer wasn't important enough to maintain eye contact.

These aren't advanced techniques. They're fundamentals. But like any fundamental skill, they need to be practiced until they become natural. A firm handshake. Eye contact during conversations. Active listening instead of just waiting for your turn to talk.

Speaking of listening, this is where a lot of leaders fail. They're so focused on talking, on being heard, that they miss crucial opportunities to listen and help others. The best leaders I've known were often the ones who talked the least but listened the most.

There's a program I often recommend that teaches people how to conduct themselves professionally. It starts with the basics: how to introduce yourself and how to handle basic business interactions. On your very first day, they make you give a five-minute introduction of yourself. Most people panic when they realize five minutes is an eternity when you're speaking publicly. But that's exactly the point—to make you conscious of these fundamental communication skills that we take for granted.

This is particularly crucial in today's world of virtual communication. When you're on video calls, these fundamentals become even more important. Your body language must be more intentional. Your eye contact (with the camera) has to be more consistent. Your listening must be more active because you can't rely on all the subtle physical cues we get in person.

But here's the most important thing I've learned about communication as a leader: You can't just communicate; you have to connect. John Maxwell wrote a book called *Everyone Communicates, Few Connect*. That title alone captures one of the most crucial distinctions in leadership. Anyone can send an email or give a presentation. But can you make people feel heard? Can you inspire them to action? Can you build trust through your communications?

That's why mastering these fundamentals is so crucial. Because when the pressure is on—when you're called on unexpectedly to speak, when you're dealing with a crisis, when you need to inspire your team—you'll default to your level of preparation. If you haven't mastered the fundamentals, no amount of fancy words will save you.

The Power of Simplicity

Let me tell you about a speech I gave at the University of North Carolina, Wilmington. The topic was cybersecurity and veteran-owned businesses—complex subjects that could fill days of discussion. But here's my secret: I didn't spend time writing out a full speech. Instead, I focused on three key themes. That's it. Just three words that guided my entire presentation.

Why three? Because simplicity is powerful. When you can take something complex and make it simple—not simplistic, but simple—you've mastered that topic. Einstein said it best: "If you can't explain it simply, you don't understand it well enough."

I see leaders mess this up all the time. They think complexity makes them sound smarter, more qualified, more "leader-like." They'll use technical jargon, complex frameworks, and elaborate PowerPoint slides. But here's what I learned at Space Command: If you can't explain your mission to someone who has no technical background, you don't really understand it yourself.

When I talk about space operations, I could throw around terms like "apogee" and "perigee" and "cislunar." That would make me sound knowledgeable to the technical folks. But what about everyone else? Instead, I focus on what matters: If space isn't operating efficiently, troops won't get their supplies, GPS won't work, and our global economy could shut down. Suddenly, everyone understands what's at stake.

This approach to simplicity isn't just about public speaking. It's about all aspects of leadership. When you're sharing your vision, giving feedback, and solving problems, the simpler and clearer you can make it, the more effective you'll be.

Here's how I apply the Rule of Three:

1. Pick three main points for any communication

2. Tell stories that illustrate those points

3. Trust that if you know your subject matter, the details will flow naturally

Each of those three points might have sub-points, but I never lose sight of the main structure. It's like building a house—you need a solid framework before you start adding all the details.

The beauty of this approach is that it helps you handle unexpected situations. If someone throws you a curveball, like when my boss once called on me with no warning to brief an ambassador, you can still deliver because you're working from fundamental principles, not memorized scripts.

When I work with young leaders, I often see them trying to prove their worth through complexity. They'll write elaborate emails when a simple conversation would do. They'll create complicated processes when a straightforward approach would work better. They're doing what I call "fighting the ghost of their own insecurity."

But true mastery shows itself in simplicity. Think about the most influential leaders you know. Chances are, they have the ability to take complex ideas and make them accessible to everyone. They don't use complexity as a shield, they use simplicity as a bridge.

Simplicity builds clarity. Clarity builds confidence. And confidence creates movement. A confused team hesitates. A clear team executes. That's why great leaders obsess over making things simple—not to look smart, but to make progress possible.

This principle extends to how you run your team. Routine matters. Doing the ordinary things extraordinarily well matters. As Pat Riley, the legendary basketball coach, said: "Excellence is the gradual result of always striving to do better." Notice he didn't say "Excellence is doing complicated things." He understood that mastery comes from doing the fundamentals exceptionally well.

Remember this: Your job as a leader isn't to prove how smart you are. It's to make sure your message is understood and your mission is accomplished. And most of the time, the simplest approach is the most effective.

The Art of Being Well-Rounded

Many CEOs today aren't the technical wizards of their companies. Steve Jobs wasn't coding iOS. Jeff Bezos isn't personally optimizing Amazon's algorithms. What sets these leaders apart isn't their technical expertise—it's their vision and their ability to understand the bigger picture. And that comes from being well-rounded.

Want to know who really understood the power of mastering fundamentals? Leonardo da Vinci. Now, most people look at the Mona Lisa or The Last Supper and see the end result—the masterpieces. What they don't see are the thousands of practice sketches in his notebooks. Pages and pages of hands. Countless studies of facial expressions. Detailed drawings of how light falls on fabric.

Before he could paint that famous smile, he had to understand the anatomy of every muscle involved in human expression. Before he could create those dramatic scenes, he had to master the basic chemistry of paint and the mathematics of perspective. He filled notebook after notebook with what most would consider boring fundamentals—the way cloth folds, the way shadows fall, the way bodies move.

Here's what gets me about Da Vinci: he was arguably one of the most brilliant minds in human history, but he never thought he was too good for the basics. Even at the height of his fame, he was still studying, still practicing, still working on fundamentals. He'd spend hours watching how water moves, sketching the same object from different angles, breaking complex things down into their simple components.

"Details make perfection," he said, "and perfection is not a detail." Think about that for a minute. He understood that mastery doesn't come from some flash of genius but from deep understanding and relentless practice of the fundamentals.

I see too many leaders trying to skip this part. They want to paint their masterpiece before they've learned to mix their colors. They want to lead complex organizations before they've mastered basic human interaction. But that's not how excellence works. Whether you're creating art or leading people, the fundamentals are what make everything else possible.

When I'm working with young leaders who are impatient to move up, and who think the basics are beneath them, I think about Da Vinci's notebooks. Even a genius had to master the fundamentals. What makes us think we can skip them?

I learned the lesson about mastering fundamentals in an unexpected place—the battlefield. When we were entering Iraq, I remember General Mattis pointing out something profound: If Napoleon saw today's battlefield, he wouldn't be surprised. Sure, the technology has evolved dramatically, but the fundamental nature of conflict remains the same. That's why being well-rounded—understanding history, human nature, and patterns of behavior—is so crucial.

Let me be clear: I'm not suggesting you shouldn't be an expert in your field. What I am saying is that expertise alone isn't enough. You need to understand the arts, appreciate culture, read widely, and stay curious about the world beyond your specialty.

Here's what I tell my teams: Always aim to be the dumbest person in the room. Not literally, of course, but adopt that mindset. Push yourself beyond your comfort zone. If you're a technical person, read a book about string theory or quantum physics. If you're a numbers person, study art history. Read science fiction; it often predicts where technology is heading before we get there.

Want some proof? I'm on a list of about 900 people who are banned for life from Russia.[12] Why? Because understanding politics, history, and human behavior allowed me to see and speak about patterns that others missed. I could connect the dots between Putin's early life experiences, like getting into a fight on a subway that derailed his KGB career, and his current leadership style. Or how China's current president applied to join the Chinese Communist Party ten times before being accepted, and how that persistence shapes his actions today.

This isn't just about collecting random facts. It's about developing the kind of contextual intelligence that lets you understand why people and organizations behave the way they do. It's about being able to draw on stories and examples from history when you're facing new challenges.

Did you know that 92% of female CEOs played team sports in college? That's not a coincidence. Team sports teach you about losing, about working with others, about resilience. These experiences shape how you lead. Every time you step outside your comfort zone to learn something new, you're adding another tool to your leadership toolkit.

I take my daughters to museums, to the theater, and to experience different cultures, not because I expect them to become art critics, but because I want them to develop the kind of well-rounded perspective that will serve them no matter what path they choose.

John F. Kennedy said it best: "Leadership and learning are indispensable to each other." That's why continuous learning isn't just a nice-to-have; it's a fundamental requirement for effective leadership. This includes:

- Formal education
- Learning from mentors
- Learning from failures
- Learning from honest feedback
- Learning from experiences outside your comfort zone

The beauty of failure and honest feedback is that they force you to grow in ways that success never could. Remember my story about asking General Neller for feedback after a presentation? Everyone else was patting me on the back, but I knew I needed that honest assessment to improve.

Being well-rounded doesn't mean being an expert at everything. It means having enough breadth of knowledge and experience to understand different perspectives, to make connections others miss, and to communicate effectively with people from all walks of life.

Let me tell you about General George Marshall, because his story perfectly illustrates something I learned in the Marine Corps about mastering fundamentals. After World War I, Marshall had his pick of prestigious positions. He'd proven himself in combat, had the right connections, and could have fast-tracked his way up the chain of command. Instead, he chose to become an instructor at the Infantry School at Fort Benning.

Think about that choice for a minute. Here's a combat-proven officer choosing to teach basic infantry tactics instead of taking a cushy Pentagon position or a high-profile command. Most of his peers thought he was crazy. In the military, just like in business, there is often pressure to move up as quickly as possible, to chase the next promotion, or to grab the high-visibility assignments.

But Marshall understood something fundamental about leadership: You can't build excellence on a shaky foundation. At Fort Benning, he didn't just teach tactics, he revolutionized how the Army trained leaders. He stripped away all the ceremonial nonsense and focused on the basics: decision-making under pressure, clear communication, and practical problem-solving.

Here's where it gets interesting. When World War II broke out, the U.S. Army had to expand from 189,000 soldiers to over 8 million. Think about that scale of growth—it's like taking a small company and turning it into Amazon overnight. But here's the thing—many of the leaders who led that expansion had come through Marshall's infantry school. Because he'd spent those years focusing on fundamentals, the Army had a solid foundation to build on.

When Marshall became U.S. Army Chief of Staff, he made a lot of controversial decisions. He fired more senior officers than any leader before him, including some long-time friends. But he had a simple criterion: Could they adapt to modern warfare? Had they mastered the fundamentals well enough to apply them in new situations?

I think about this a lot in today's military, especially when dealing with space and cyber operations. The technology changes constantly, but the fundamentals of leadership remain the same. The ability to make decisions under pressure, to communicate clearly, to solve complex problems—these are the foundations on which everything else is built.

Marshall understood something that too many leaders forget: Position doesn't make you a leader. Mastering fundamentals does. When I see leaders struggling today, it's often not because they lack intelligence or creativity. It's because they skipped over the basics in their rush to the top.

That's why I tell my teams: Don't worry about the next promotion. Don't chase the high-profile assignments. Focus on mastering the fundamentals. Because when the real challenges come—and they will come—that's what you'll fall back on.

When everything's on the line, you don't rise to the occasion, you fall back on your level of preparation. That's why mastering the basics isn't optional. It's the difference between confidence and collapse when pressure hits.

The Art of Reading the Room

In the '80s when I first watched martial arts movies, I couldn't figure out why Bruce Lee's lips didn't match what he was saying. I had no idea about dubbing back then. But it taught me something crucial about leadership: When things don't line up—when what you're seeing doesn't match what you're hearing—people notice. This is what we call the audio not matching the video.

This is where emotional intelligence comes in. It's not just about being nice or empathetic (though those things matter). It's about having the awareness to read situations and adjust your approach accordingly. Being emotionally intelligent doesn't mean you're weak; it means you're smart enough to put yourself in other people's shoes.

I've had to speak to elementary school students and elected officials, often in the same week. The information might be similar, but the delivery must be completely different. That's not about dumbing things down; it's about being smart enough to meet people where they are. Know your audience and speak to their needs.

This kind of versatility in leadership styles is crucial. Sometimes you need to be more adaptable, sometimes collaborative. Sometimes you need to be a visionary, and sometimes a practical problem-solver. The key is knowing which approach fits the situation, and that comes from being able to read the room, feel the energy, and understand what they're saying through their body language.

One of my mentors once told me: "Leaders who are talking all the time miss things." They leave gaps in finding opportunities to help others because they're so focused on being heard that they forget to listen. Real emotional intelligence starts with shutting up and paying attention. I always say there's a reason we have two ears and one mouth: Listening is more important than talking.

Here's what I've learned about developing this skill:

- Watch body language, both yours and others'
- Pay attention to what's not being said
- Notice energy shifts in the room
- Listen for underlying concerns
- Adapt your approach based on what you observe

This isn't manipulation, it's understanding. It's about being aware enough to know when someone needs encouragement versus when they need direct feedback. When a team needs inspiration versus when they need clear direction.

I see a lot of leaders trying to adopt a one-size-fits-all approach. They find a leadership style that worked once and stick to it religiously. But that's like having only one club in your golf bag. Sure, you might get really good at using that one club, but you're going to struggle on most of the course.

True emotional intelligence means having range—being able to flex your leadership style based on what the situation and people need. Sometimes that means being a tough, decisive leader. Other times it means being a supportive mentor. The key is knowing which version of yourself the moment calls for.

This might sound exhausting, having to constantly read situations and adjust your approach. But once you master these fundamentals, they become second nature. Just like a good athlete doesn't have to think about basic form during a game, a good leader doesn't have to consciously think about reading the room; they just do it.

You're not trying to be all things to all people. You're trying to be the right leader for each situation. That's what emotional intelligence in leadership is about.

The Art of Adaptation

Einstein put it perfectly: "The measure of intelligence is the ability to change." In today's rapidly evolving world, the ability to adapt, to learn, to see the bigger picture isn't just helpful, it's essential for survival.

Every morning when I get up to make my girls breakfast, I'm reminded that no day is exactly like the one before. Sometimes they wake up ready to take on the world. Sometimes they've been up since

3 a.m. with nightmares. Each situation requires a different kind of leadership, even if the goal of getting everyone fed and off to school remains the same.

The same principle applies to organizational leadership. I remember a situation at Space Command that perfectly illustrates this. We were developing our operations plan, dealing with complex scenarios about how to protect space assets and provide capabilities to ground forces. The technical aspects were challenging enough, but the real test was adapting my communication style to different audiences.

When I briefed the technical teams, they wanted the deep details. When I briefed senior leadership, they needed the strategic implications. When I talked to our international partners, I had to focus on shared objectives and collaborative opportunities. Same information, but three entirely different approaches.

Look at what happened to Circuit City while Best Buy adapted and survived. Circuit City couldn't adapt to changing consumer habits and new technologies. They stuck to what they knew until what they knew became obsolete.

The ability to adapt isn't just about responding to external changes. It's about actively seeking ways to evolve and improve. When I was developing our training programs at Space Command, I made it clear to my team that the only thing that would get them in trouble was sticking to "the way we've always done it." Innovation doesn't come from comfort zones.

Think about the most significant challenges in your organization right now. Are they technical problems? Maybe. But more likely, they're adaptive challenges—situations where the old solutions don't work anymore, where you need to think differently and lead differently.

I learned this lesson early in my career. As an intelligence analyst, I was trained to look for patterns, to anticipate threats, and to understand capabilities. But as I moved into leadership positions, I realized that technical expertise alone wasn't enough. I had to adapt my approach based on who I was leading, what they needed, and what the situation demanded.

This kind of adaptability requires humility. You must be willing to admit that your preferred way of doing things might not be the best way for every situation. It requires the emotional intelligence to read the room and the flexibility to adjust your approach. Most importantly, it requires the wisdom to know when to hold firm on principles and when to be flexible on methods. I've often used Kenny Rogers' song "The Gambler" as a lesson in leadership:

> *Know when to fold 'em*
> *Know when to walk away*
> *And know when to run...*

Leaders today need extreme adaptability. Not just the ability to weather changes, but the ability to thrive through them. To see challenges as opportunities for innovation rather than threats to the status quo.

The Foundation of Well-being

When I talk about mastering fundamentals, I often get questions about technical skills, leadership techniques, and communication strategies. But there is an even more basic foundation that too many leaders ignore: their own physical and mental well-being.

I learned this lesson the hard way. A few years back, I watched a presentation about eating well and forming healthy habits that was given to government employees. The irony wasn't lost on anyone in the room—the person speaking about nutrition was visibly obese. The disconnect between the message and the messenger completely undermined their credibility.

This isn't about perfect fitness or winning bodybuilding competitions. It's about something more fundamental: As a leader, you're asking people to follow your example. If you're not taking care of yourself, what message are you sending about taking care of your team?

In my career, I've seen how physical well-being directly impacts leadership effectiveness. When I'm well-rested, when I'm physically active, when I'm eating right, I make better decisions. I communicate more clearly. I handle stress more effectively. It's not complicated, but it is fundamental.

The same goes for mental well-being. Leadership can be incredibly isolating, especially at higher levels. You're dealing with sensitive information, making tough decisions, carrying burdens you can't always share. If you don't have a strong foundation of mental wellness, these pressures can break you and they will rest on your shoulders like a heavy backpack.

I tell my leaders to think of it like maintaining a vehicle. You wouldn't expect your car to run without regular maintenance, without checking the oil, without filling the tank. Yet somehow, we expect ourselves to perform at peak levels without taking care of our basic needs.

Accountability and integrity start here. If you can't be accountable for your own well-being, how can you be accountable for a team's? If you can't maintain integrity in your personal habits, how can you maintain it in your leadership?

This isn't just about being healthy for health's sake. It's about building the physical and mental resilience you need to lead effectively. When a crisis hits—and it will hit—you need to have the stamina to handle it. When your team needs you to be at your best— and they will—you need to have the energy to deliver.

The best leaders I've known had this figured out. They understood that taking care of themselves wasn't selfish, it was necessary. They made time for exercise, for proper rest, for mental breaks. Not because they had extra time, but because they knew these things were fundamental to their effectiveness as leaders. This is about prioritization; you can't redline forever.

Think of it this way: Your physical and mental well being are part of your leadership infrastructure. Just as you wouldn't build a skyscraper on a weak foundation, you can't build strong leadership on a neglected personal foundation.

This isn't about perfection. It's about progression. It's about setting an example through your actions, not just your words. Because at the end of the day, people don't follow what you say, they follow what you do.

Looking Ahead: From Fundamentals to Impact

When I think back to that kid who graduated last in his Intel school class, I'm reminded that mastering fundamentals isn't a one-time achievement. It's a continuous journey. Every time I think I've got it figured out, every time I start feeling comfortable, life has a way of showing me there's more to learn.

The fundamentals we've covered in this chapter, from decision-making to communication, from adaptability to personal well-being, might seem basic. But like any foundation, they determine what you can build on top of them. The stronger your grasp of these fundamentals, the higher you can reach as a leader.

Think about my friend Josh again, the one who started out flipping burgers and now owns eleven restaurants. His success didn't come from some revolutionary new approach to fast food. It came from understanding and mastering the fundamentals of his business from the ground up. That's what allowed him to navigate challenges like COVID-19, market fluctuations, and management issues. When you truly understand the basics, you can handle almost any curveball life throws at you.

As we move into the next chapter about fueling the fire and why drive outpaces grit, remember this: The fundamentals aren't something you master once and move on from. They're something you return to again and again, each time understanding them at a deeper level.

I see it in my own leadership journey every day. Whether I'm briefing an ambassador with no notice or helping my daughters understand why character matters, it always comes back to the fundamentals. Did I make eye contact? Did I listen actively? Did I communicate clearly? Did I lead by example?

Your journey forward from here isn't about adding more complexity, it's about achieving deeper mastery of these basics. About doing ordinary things extraordinarily well. About building such a solid foundation that you can handle whatever challenges come your way.

The fundamentals you master today don't just make you a better leader. They become part of your legacy. Long after you've moved on, people will still remember how you made decisions, how you listened, and how you showed up. They'll carry those habits forward into their own leadership. That's the power of fundamentals—they ripple outward, shaping teams, culture, and the leaders who come after you.

So, when you commit to mastering the basics, you're not just improving yourself but setting a standard others will build on. And that's what real leadership is about.

Leadership Fundamentals Baseline Drill

Before we move into the action steps, I want to leave you with something simple but powerful, a baseline drill for leadership fundamentals. Think of it like your daily leadership workout. These aren't glamorous. They don't come with awards or applause. But done consistently, they'll build the kind of foundation you can trust under pressure.

Do these daily:

- Make eye contact and remember someone's name.
- Give one piece of specific, sincere feedback.
- Ask one high-quality question in a meeting or conversation.
- Make one decision you've been putting off.
- Reflect on one lesson from the day before.

Do these five things daily and you're no longer guessing. You're training. Mastery doesn't come from motion. It comes from deliberate movement, done consistently over time.

Taking Action

Start by being honest with yourself about your fundamental skills. Where are you strong? In what areas do you need work? Remember, this isn't about judgment, it's about growth.

Make regular time to practice communication basics. Have real conversations. Look people in the eye. Remember names. These aren't small things; they're the building blocks of leadership. For example, write thank you notes with something specific about your relationship or engagement.

Invest in your well-being. Not because it's trendy, but because it's necessary. You can't lead others effectively if you're running on empty yourself.

Stay curious. Read widely. Learn about topics outside your expertise. The broader your understanding, the more connections you can make, and the better leader you'll be.

Most importantly, remember that mastering fundamentals isn't about reaching some final destination. It's about committing to the journey of continuous improvement. About doing the basic things better each day than you did the day before.

Because at the end of the day, leadership isn't about knowing everything; it's about building a foundation strong enough to support whatever challenges come your way. Master the fundamentals, and everything else becomes possible.

CHAPTER TAKEAWAYS

- **Communication fundamentals matter:** Only 7% of your message comes from words; the rest is tone, body language, and presence. Master these before focusing on advanced techniques.

- **Simplicity is key:** If you can't explain your vision in three key points, you may not understand it well enough. Great leaders make the complex understandable.

- **Be well-rounded:** Leadership problems are multi-faceted. The broader your knowledge—across arts, science, and history—the more tools you'll have to solve them.

- **Emotional intelligence and adaptability are critical:** They're not "soft skills"; they're essential for survival. Learn to read the room, adapt your style, and connect with others.

- **Well-being is part of leadership:** Physical and mental well-being aren't optional, they're fundamental. A leader who doesn't care for themselves can't expect others to follow.

*"The purpose of life
is a life of purpose."*
— Robert Byrne

— 5 —

BEYOND GRIT: WHY DRIVE LEADS TO LASTING SUCCESS

Here's something they don't tell you in leadership books: Sometimes your worst failure becomes your biggest wake-up call.

I graduated dead last in my intelligence school class. Dead. Last. And it wasn't because I wasn't capable. It was because I walked in with the amount of arrogance you would expect from maybe a Steve Jobs or a trillionaire—just complete, misplaced arrogance for an 18-year-old boy. I put in zero effort, thinking it didn't matter.

To understand how spectacular this failure was, you need to know what Intel School means in the Marine Corps. This isn't just any training; it's where you learn to be an intelligence analyst, to process everything from satellite information to human intelligence, synthesizing it all to give commanders the battlefield picture they need. Lives literally depend on doing this job well.

But there I was, a cocky kid who'd skated through high school early, thinking I was above it all. The Marine Corps had a different opinion. Not only did I graduate last, but I also nearly didn't graduate at all. If it hadn't been for some leadership intervention, I probably would have been reassigned to a different specialty entirely.

In that moment, as I stood there as the last-ranked graduate, reality hit me hard. I realized I was on a path to mediocrity at best. I tell people now that I was headed straight toward living underneath a bridge.

This is where most people would talk about grit, about how they buckled down and pushed through. But what happened next wasn't about grit. It was about drive. The difference is fundamental to leadership development.

Drive is proactive, born from self-reflection and vision. It involves taking time to understand yourself, formulating a deliberate plan, and executing with purpose. While grit responds to challenges as they emerge, drive anticipates and shapes the path ahead. Grit would have gotten me through the next assignment, focusing on perseverance in the face of difficulty, helping me to weather the storms. Drive, however, compelled me to envision excellence beyond mere survival and pursue it relentlessly.

Drive charts the course that others follow. Both qualities are valuable, but drive transforms potential into extraordinary achievement through its forward-looking, visionary nature. I've learned throughout my career that drive is more important than grit. While both matter, drive is proactive—it's about seeing where you want to go and charting the course to get there. Grit is reactive—it's about persevering through whatever comes your way. You need both, but without drive, you're just enduring rather than advancing.

Drive is what took me from that embarrassed last-place graduate to becoming the first Marine to serve as the command senior enlisted leader of the Defense Intelligence Agency, United States Cyber Command, United States Space Command, and the second Marine to serve as the command senior enlisted leader for the National Security Agency. That transformation didn't happen because I gritted my teeth and endured. It happened because that failure lit a fire inside me—a drive not just to survive, but to excel.

That's the moment I stopped aiming for average and started chasing mastery. Drive didn't just get me back on course, it forced me to redefine the course entirely. And once you get a taste of what it feels like to be driven, survival mode will never be enough again.

Drive: The Proactive Edge

Drive manifests in concrete ways that distinguish truly exceptional leaders. While determination is common among achievers, drive operates at a higher level—it infuses every decision with strategic intent and creates momentum before obstacles appear. It's the difference between the runner who trains solely for the race and the athlete who builds a comprehensive development system that transforms their entire approach to competition. Drive doesn't just overcome barriers; it anticipates and transforms them into opportunities for advancement on your leadership journey.

Drive is what pushes you to think beyond the immediate challenge. It helps you guide decision-making and strategy. Most importantly, it allows you to effectively communicate your vision to your team. When you're driven, others can see themselves in your vision. It provides clarity and focus that mere determination can't match.

I learned this lesson most powerfully during my time in intel school, though not in the way you might think. Remember that arrogant kid who graduated dead last? That was grit's failure. I had the determination to stick it out, sure. But I lacked the drive to excel, to push beyond mere survival. I hadn't yet developed that internal fire that makes you want to be better, not just good enough.

Drive creates a roadmap that extends far beyond immediate obstacles. Once, during my time at USSC, we were working on our operations plan—essentially, what we would do in case of emergency. This wasn't just about reacting to hypothetical threats; it required a comprehensive vision of potential futures. As the senior enlisted leader, I watched officers struggling with technical jargon that others couldn't understand. They were talking to other space professionals about apogee, perigee, and cislunar concepts—terminology that left many nodding off or mentally checking out.

I took a different approach. Rather than focusing on technical specifications, I emphasized the real-world impact: "If space isn't operating efficiently, you won't get logistical supplies to the battlefield. You won't be able to use GPS. Our global economy would shut down." This long-term, big-picture thinking is what drive produces—the ability to connect immediate actions to far-reaching consequences that everyone can understand.

Drive means building frameworks that anticipate change rather than merely responding to it. When I served as the intelligence chief for Marine Special Operations Command, I could hand-select 383 professionals, what I called "meat-eating assassins"—all combat veterans who excelled at their jobs. Yet having this talented team wasn't enough. Drive pushed me to develop systems that would sustain excellence regardless of personnel changes or mission shifts. Without that forward-looking perspective, we'd be constantly reacting rather than shaping events.

As General Mattis once said about our operations in Iraq, "If Napoleon saw the battlefield today, he wouldn't be surprised. Although technology has evolved, the conflict has happened before." Drive helps you see these patterns and prepare for them before they emerge, giving you a decisive advantage that reactive approaches simply cannot provide.

You see this in the military too. No one comes in as a four-star general. Everyone starts at the bottom, mastering the basics and fundamentals. What separates those who rise through the ranks isn't just their ability to endure hardship, it's their drive to learn, to grow, and to become better with each challenge.

And here's the truth: Some people rise fast because of opportunity, but the ones who last are the ones who are driven. Drive keeps you moving forward long after the applause has faded and the spotlight's moved on. It's the difference between peaking early and becoming the one others study later.

—

I've got a buddy named Ed, an Air Force veteran, my closest friend, and the kind of guy I joke should've been a Marine. Even as a civilian, he volunteered for a combat tour in Iraq because sitting on the sidelines just wasn't in his DNA. Ed is pure grit. We've played golf together in rain so heavy you'd think Noah's Ark might float by, and the man won't flinch. He won't quit. He won't even acknowledge the conditions. He just keeps swinging.

Ed reminds me that grit isn't loud—it's quiet, consistent, and immovable. And while this chapter is about drive, I'd be lying if I said grit doesn't matter. It's what keeps you on the path when the drive wavers. And if you're lucky, you'll have an Ed in your life—someone whose presence alone raises your standard. When I think about longevity in leadership, I think of him. Because showing up again and again, regardless of the weather, is something you can build a life and a legacy on.

Vision: Where Drive Meets Direction

According to the Self-Determination Theory—and yes, there is actual science behind this—people are motivated by intrinsic factors like autonomy, mastery, and purpose. When you align your efforts with these internal desires, you're more likely to achieve long-term success than if you're just gritting your teeth and pushing through.

Recently, I was working with a female colleague who had achieved a very senior leadership position in the Air Force. Some anonymous critics suggested she'd earned her position "laying on her back." Now, grit would tell you to ignore the trolls and keep pushing forward. But drive? Drive takes a different approach.

As I told her, "Has Michael Jordan ever responded to a negative comment on social media?" Of course not. Winners focus on winning; losers focus on winners. When you're truly driven, you don't have time to validate or elevate those beneath you by lowering yourself to their conversation.

This isn't just motivational talk, it's practical leadership strategy. When you tell your team they need to achieve 10% growth next month, they'll smell any doubt in your voice. You have to visualize it and believe it first. Otherwise, you won't be authentic, and they'll sense your fear and uncertainty.

Henry Ford's familiar quote certainly applies here: "Whether you think you can or you think you can't, you're right." Leaders need to understand that the greatest obstacles they face are almost always internal. It's the ceiling you place on yourself that limits your growth.

Here's a question I often ask leaders: What does success look like to you next month? Next year? Five years from now? If you can't explain your plan to a group of five-year-olds, you haven't clarified it enough. Get rid of the jargon, strip away the acronyms. Make it clear enough that anyone can understand and connect with your vision.

The saying "High tide raises all boats" isn't just a nice platitude. When your drive is powered by your morals, values, character, and sense of purpose, it lifts everyone around you. Think about Viktor Frankl's insights in *Man's Search for Meaning*: knowing your why and your purpose is what fuels sustainable drive.

Frankl's perspective carries extraordinary weight because he developed it under the most horrific circumstances imaginable. As a Holocaust survivor who endured years in Nazi concentration camps including Auschwitz, Frankl observed something remarkable: Those who maintained a sense of purpose—who could envision a future beyond their present suffering—were more likely to survive. Despite starvation, torture, and witnessing unimaginable brutality, Frankl discovered that "those who have a 'why' to live can bear almost any 'how.'"[13]

This profound insight applies directly to leadership drive. When your purpose transcends mere advancement or achievement, when it connects to values larger than yourself, your drive becomes nearly unbreakable. In my military career, I've seen colleagues burn out pursuing promotions, while others maintained unwavering energy in serving a mission they deeply believed in. The difference wasn't intelligence or talent, but rather the foundation upon which their drive was built.

But here's the critical part: Drive without action is just daydreaming. Success isn't doing something once; it's consistent, repeated action. Take something as simple as putting your gym bag in your car the night before, or getting your kids' stuff ready for school. These small acts of preparation, driven by a clear vision of what you want to achieve, lead to exponential results in growth and achievement.

Cultivating Your Internal Fire

Drive isn't an inherent trait that some leaders possess and others don't. It can be deliberately developed. The military taught me that drive emerges when personal goals align with meaningful purpose. I've seen this repeatedly: When Marines understand how their specific role supports the broader mission, their performance transforms. The same principle applies in any leadership context.

People often ask me, "Scott, why are you so driven?" And honestly, sometimes I can't answer. Is it because I'm driven not to be like my father? Is it because I'm still chasing that "Well done" I never heard growing up? Or is it just who I've become?

Maybe it's all of that. Or maybe drive is just the scar tissue from every time I was underestimated—every time someone overlooked me, out-ranked me, or doubted I belonged in the room. I don't carry that as bitterness, I carry it as fuel. The chip on my shoulder isn't weight. It's propulsion.

And over time, that drive doesn't just push you. It shapes you into someone who refuses to settle for "good enough," even when nobody's watching.

Because drive, at its core, isn't about the spotlight. It's about what you do in the dark, when no one's clapping, and quitting would be easier.

When I took the position at Space Command, I had the option to maintain the status quo. Instead, I told my commander, "You're going to have to tell me to slow down." We built a plan, we went after the gaps, and we transformed how we developed our people. That wasn't just about working hard, it was about having a vision and being driven to achieve it.

Here's how you cultivate that kind of drive:

First, you must identify what deeply motivates you. And I'm not talking about surface-level stuff like bonuses or promotions. I'm talking about the core drives that get you up in the morning, even when everything's going wrong.

Second, you need to actively seek challenges that promote growth. When you have an opportunity to take on a tough assignment in the military, I always say take it. Go to the unit that's most messed up and fix it. That's the mark of a real leader—someone driven not just to succeed but to make things better.

When I speak at universities now, I don't focus my preparation time on writing out a speech or memorizing lines because I've learned that when you're driven by purpose rather than just trying to get through it, you need a different approach. I keep it simple: I focus on three key themes and let the stories flow naturally.

The distinction becomes clearest in high-pressure moments. As

I have said, when I prepare for critical briefings, I focus on mastering three key themes rather than memorizing a script. This approach reflects the fundamental difference between drive and grit. Grit manifests as rigid adherence to prepared remarks—pushing through word by word regardless of audience response. Drive, however, creates the mental freedom to prioritize connection and impact. It allows me to read the room, adjust in real-time, and ensure every person understands why the information matters. This flexibility stems from confidence in your purpose, not just your preparation.

I explain this approach to people like we're preparing for a standup comedy routine. You must read the room, understand the cultural references, and know your audience. When I had a sparse crowd in DC once, I made a joke about it. Why? Because drive isn't about perfectly executing a plan, it's about creating real connections, about making an impact that lasts beyond your time on stage.

Many misunderstand drive as uninterrupted forward momentum, but my own journey proves otherwise. In 2012, severe back problems nearly ended my military career. The prescribed OxyContin left me feeling disconnected—essentially watching my own life from a distance. The pain and medication affected me so profoundly that I approached my boss to initiate retirement paperwork. I couldn't maintain Marine Corps standards, and rather than compromise those standards, I prepared to leave the service I loved. Drive isn't about avoiding these valleys, it's about how you navigate through them.

Instead of giving up, I found what's called the PERRES program: Performance and Resilience. Within three years, I went from barely being able to function to competing in amateur powerlifting competitions. That wasn't grit. That wasn't just pushing through pain. That was drive: seeing a better future and being pulled toward it.

Grit might have kept me on the couch, enduring the pain. Drive pulled me off it and toward something better. That's the power of vision-backed effort—it doesn't just push through, it pulls forward with purpose.

The old man at the beach in a Speedo doesn't care what anyone thinks about him. That's freedom. That's what happens when you're driven by internal standards rather than external judgments. Winners don't focus on losers. When you're truly driven, you don't have time to worry about what others think because you're too busy becoming who you're meant to be.

Breaking Through Mental Barriers

In the military, a horribly outdated, rigid, hierarchical Napoleonic rank structure tells you exactly what your rank does and doesn't allow. It's a perfect example of how we often put artificial ceilings on ourselves. But drive? Drive doesn't care about artificial ceilings.

Mental barriers can limit drive more effectively than any external obstacle. This became painfully clear in 2012 while serving as an Intel chief at Camp Lejeune. After wearing the master gunnery sergeant E9 rank for two years, I received orders to deliver a presentation at Special Operations headquarters. Despite my position and experience, internal doubts began to surface as I prepared for this high-visibility assignment.

On day one, during the icebreakers, I looked around the room. Everyone was older, and more weathered—Navy SEALs, Marine

Raiders, Green Berets. They all looked like they'd stepped out of a movie about hardened warriors. And there I was, looking younger than most of them.

So, I drove to the little exchange store on base, looking for Just For Men hair dye. I wanted to add some gray to my hair to look older. Yes, I had a massive case of imposter syndrome that day.

Here's the ridiculous part—they don't make products to *add* gray to your hair. Every product is designed to cover it up. But I was so worried about appearances that I wasn't focusing on what really mattered: the substance of what I had to share.

The next day, I gave my presentation. And those seasoned operators came up afterward to congratulate me, to tell me how valuable the information was. They didn't care that I looked younger. They didn't care that I didn't have as many combat ribbons. They cared about competence.

What I learned that day is that most mature professionals just want people who can deliver. They're not counting your gray hairs or measuring your biceps. They're measuring your impact.

Drive is what made me realize those insecurities were irrelevant to the mission. Drive keeps you focused on what matters.

Consider the Wright brothers versus Samuel Pierpont Langley in the race for powered flight. Langley had everything going for him—government backing with a $50,000 grant (enormous in 1898), a prestigious role at the Smithsonian, access to elite scientists, and the media cheering him on. He built his flying machine in secrecy, rolled it out with fanfare, and when it crashed, he blamed everyone else. Then he quit. That's grit without drive: pushing forward until the moment the spotlight dims or the plan breaks.

Meanwhile, the Wright brothers, two unknown bicycle mechanics from Dayton, Ohio, had no grants. No elite education. No fanfare. But they had something Langley didn't: drive. They had a vision so clear they would risk everything to make it real. They studied birds. They built their own wind tunnel to test theories Langley never questioned. They failed quietly, rebuilt obsessively, and learned constantly. And when they succeeded in 1903, flying 120 feet at Kitty Hawk, Langley didn't congratulate them; he disappeared from the conversation entirely.

The Wrights weren't in it for recognition. They were driven to solve a problem no one else could. And that's why they succeeded. Not just because they worked hard, but because they saw further.

That's what drive looks like. It isn't louder. It's longer-lasting. It's vision-backed grit with an engine behind it.

In today's world, we're building resilience in all sorts of ways. I'm building it into my business planning—I know I've got about two to four more years where consulting will be viable for me. After that, inevitably, newer people from the defense community will be hotter commodities. That's not pessimism, that's reality. And drive means planning for that reality now, thinking five to 10 years down the road.

Whether it's technology, intelligence, or leadership itself, the world keeps evolving. You can either fight it like Kodak fought digital cameras (which they actually invented but were afraid would destroy their business), or you can drive forward into the future, anticipating and adapting to change.

What fuels drive is the clarity that comes from knowing where you're going and why it matters. Everything else—the self-doubt, the imposter syndrome, the artificial barriers—falls away when your drive is aligned with a clear purpose.

Looking Forward and Building Legacy

Drive isn't just about pushing toward your next goal. It's about creating lasting impact. I consult for a company right now that doesn't pay me exceptionally well. I could leave and probably make a lot more elsewhere. But I'll never leave them because of how their CEO leads—how he mentors, molds, and advises his people. He leads that organization with love, and everyone who works for him, even those who've moved on to other opportunities, would do anything for him.

That's the kind of legacy that drive, and not just grit, creates. It's not about grinding through each day; it's about building something that lasts.

Consider Admiral Hyman Rickover, known as the "Father of the Nuclear Navy." In 1947, while most naval officers were still focused on traditional ship propulsion, Rickover had the drive to envision an entirely different future. Despite massive institutional resistance, he drove the development of nuclear-powered submarines, fundamentally transforming naval warfare. It wasn't just grit that made this happen; plenty of officers had grit. It was Rickover's drive to push beyond accepted limitations, to see possibilities others couldn't yet imagine.

This kind of forward-thinking drive is crucial in today's rapidly evolving world. Take what I'm seeing in the defense and intelligence community. Technologies like CRISPR are allowing us to edit DNA. I tell my teams that massive changes are coming—you can't fight them, but you can prepare for them.

As I discussed earlier about my time at Space Command, the leaders there talked to others as if they were "in the club," using technical jargon while watching their audience mentally check out, had grit. They'd worked hard to master their technical knowledge, but they lacked the drive to connect, to make their message matter to everyone in the room. That's the difference between just maintaining expertise and driving actual change.

The secret of change, as Socrates said, is to focus all your energy not on fighting the old, but on building the new. This is ultimately why drive matters more than grit. Grit might help you protect what you have, but drive pushes you to create what could be.

The future will include artificial intelligence. We will continue to explore space. The pharmaceutical industry will keep evolving. The sun will keep rising in the east and setting in the west. These things are inevitable. You can either be driven to help shape that future, or you can grit your teeth and try to hold onto the past. The choice is yours.

That's what this chapter is about. Not just getting through, *but driving forward.* Because grit may get you to the door, but drive is what kicks it open, walks through, and builds something that lasts on the other side.

Drive Activation Drill — Do These Weekly:

- Visualize success and write down your "why" in one sentence.
- Identify one barrier you're placing on yourself, and remove it.

- Take one bold step toward a long-term goal, even if it scares you.
- Help one person connect to *their* deeper purpose.
- Revisit your mission and ask: Is this still worth the drive? Remember: Grit shows up when it's hard. Drive shows up *before it's even needed.*

CHAPTER TAKEAWAYS

- Legacy isn't built by those who just outlast others, it's built by those who out-vision them.
- Drive is about an impact that echoes. It's the mark you leave behind, not the medal you wear in the moment. When you lead with drive, you're not just climbing the ladder, you're building one for others to climb, too.
- Drive is proactive while grit is reactive; visualize your success before the challenge arrives.
- Winners focus on winning, not on responding to critics or naysayers. Don't validate negativity by engaging with it.
- The greatest obstacles to success are internal; your drive must be stronger than your self-imposed limitations.
- True drive comes from alignment with a deeper purpose. It's not just about working harder; it's about seeing further.
- Leadership isn't about existing skills but about driving toward continuous growth. Prepare for changes before they're needed.

At the professional level—whether it's sports, business, or leadership—talent gets you in the door, but drive is what keeps you on the team. I think about this often when it comes to drafting athletes out of college. Everyone in the draft is talented. What I want to know is, who is the hardest-working athlete? Who's going to show up early, stay late, and obsess over getting better? Drive separates the all-stars from the benchwarmers—not talent.

The same applies in the private sector. When I'm hiring, I'm not looking for SAT scores or polished résumés. I'm scanning for evidence of internal fire—someone who's hungry to do more than the minimum. It might be buried in a letter of recommendation or hidden in a story about their first job. But if I see that glimmer of drive, that's someone I'll bet on. Because skills can be trained, but drive can't be faked.

— 6 —

CHARTING YOUR COURSE: CRAFTING A PERSONAL LEADERSHIP VISION

I have seen senior leaders stand up and deliver technically brilliant presentations, packed with insider terminology and complex concepts. I have also seen the audience's eyes glaze over at these same presentations, their minds no doubt drifting to what they might have for lunch.

It wasn't that these leaders lacked vision; they had it in spades. The problem was they couldn't translate that vision into something their people could grab onto and run with. They were speaking their own language, not their audience's language.

You can have the most brilliant plan in the world, but if people can't understand it—or worse, don't care—you've already failed. Vision isn't about complexity. It's about clarity that invites people to act.

This reminded me of something Abraham Lincoln once grasped that many leaders still struggle with today. During the Civil War, Lincoln had to communicate one of the most complex visions imaginable—preserving not just the Union's territory, but its very soul. He could have buried this message in political jargon or military strategy. Instead, he gave us "government of the people, by the people, for the people." In fact, he said it in only 271 words. Simple. Clear. Powerful. Everyone from farmers to generals could understand and rally behind it.

But before you can share a vision, you need to define one for yourself. That means asking the hard questions: What do I stand for? What kind of impact do I want to make? What's the mark I want to leave behind? The clarity you find in those answers becomes your compass. Everything else—your goals, your communication, your leadership style—flows from that point of purpose.

That's what real vision is about—not just having a clear picture in your own mind but being able to paint that picture in ways that inspire others to see it too. It's about creating context that resonates with your audience, whether you're talking to a room full of technical experts or a team of fresh recruits.

I learned this lesson the hard way. Early in my career, I'd try to impress people with my knowledge, packing presentations with every acronym and technical term I knew. Sure, I sounded smart—to myself. But I wasn't connecting. I wasn't leading. I was just talking.

The truth about vision in leadership is this: If your people can't understand it, can't connect with it, or can't see themselves in it, it doesn't matter how brilliant it is. It's just noise. I learned this lesson early from my fourth-grade math teacher, Mrs. Hamanaka. While things weren't going well at home, she gave me a vision of what I could become that I actually understood. She saw potential in me that I couldn't see myself. I'll always be grateful to her.

That's the first time I realized vision could be given—transferred. And it might come from someone you least expect. Leaders who understand this don't just motivate. They multiply belief in others.

Years later, I faced this challenge again during the births of my three daughters—one during a massive earthquake that I almost missed because I was in Alaska, another during COVID-19, and the third who arrived six weeks early and required a month in the NICU on oxygen. Each crisis demanded clarity of vision and purpose when everything else was chaos. Through these personal challenges, I discovered that effective vision cuts through complexity and connects on a human level, just like Mrs. Hamanaka did for me all those years ago.

When we don't take the time to develop a clear, ethical vision that goes beyond immediate convenience or self-interest, we make decisions that might solve short-term problems but create long-term issues with trust and credibility.

Vision Through Core Values: The Nimitz Example

When we talk about aligning vision with values, there's no better example than Admiral Chester Nimitz's leadership in the Pacific during World War II. After Pearl Harbor, Nimitz inherited a devastating situation: a demoralized fleet, a string of defeats, and an enemy that seemed unstoppable. But what he did next demonstrates how core values shape effective vision.

Nimitz built his strategy on three fundamental values: trust in his people, commitment to calculated risk-taking, and unwavering focus on long-term objectives.[14] Unlike many leaders who try to centralize control during crises, Nimitz gave his commanders significant autonomy. He trusted them to make decisions based on his clear vision while adapting to conditions on the ground.

Consider how he handled the Battle of Midway. Intelligence suggested a major Japanese attack was coming, but there was fierce debate about the target. Nimitz trusted his intelligence team's analysis over more senior officers' opinions,[15] demonstrating how values-based leadership means backing your people when evidence supports their position, regardless of rank.

This connects directly to what I tell young leaders today: Your vision has to align with your core values or it won't survive first contact with reality. Nimitz didn't just talk about trusting his people, he demonstrated it through actions, even when those actions carried enormous risk.

Here's what's crucial about Nimitz's approach: he never let short-term setbacks derail his long-term vision. After early defeats, many wanted to adopt a defensive posture. But Nimitz understood that his core value of calculated risk-taking meant maintaining an offensive mindset while building carefully toward decisive encounters.[16]

I've seen this same principle play out in modern leadership contexts. When I was developing our intelligence strategies, I had to balance immediate tactical needs with long-term capability development. Like Nimitz, I found that staying true to core values, particularly trust in our people and commitment to long-term objectives, helped maintain clarity of vision even during crisis moments.

That's the real test of vision—it either sharpens under stress or falls apart.

That's where values do their real work—not just inspiring vision but anchoring it. I've sat in rooms at DIA, Cyber Command, and Space Command where the pressure was intense and the stakes were historic. What kept our decisions grounded wasn't a catchy strategy document but clarity on what mattered: integrity, mission, and people. When politics or pressure tried to shift the focus, it was our values that kept the vision steady. And when the world changed—as it always does—it was those same values that helped us evolve wisely, not react blindly.

And when the noise is loudest, people don't want charisma. They want clarity.

Let me give you a personal example. When I took on the role of senior enlisted leader, I had plenty of technical expertise and operational experience. But what really mattered, what made all the difference, was the clarity of my values and vision. I knew I wanted to build an organization where every member, regardless of rank or position, understood their vital role in our mission. Where technical excellence was matched by genuine care for our people.

This wasn't just some feel-good mission statement to hang on the wall. It was a deeply held conviction that shaped every decision, every interaction, every policy. Just like Perkins didn't merely want better laws; she wanted to fundamentally transform how America treated its workers.

Look at Gandhi's approach to leadership. His vision of Indian independence wasn't just about political change; it was rooted in core values of non-violence and self-reliance. These values weren't just principles he preached. They were guidelines that informed every strategic decision he made. That's what made his leadership so powerful—the absolute alignment between his values and his actions.

Nelson Mandela demonstrated this same principle from his prison cell on Robben Island. His vision for a unified South Africa never wavered because it was anchored in his core values of reconciliation and dignity for all. Even in the darkest moments, those values served as his moral compass.

But here's the thing about values and vision: they're not just for world-changing movements or national leaders. They're just as crucial for leading a small team or running a local organization. I learned this lesson watching my daughter's school principal handle a particularly challenging situation recently.

Several parents were pushing for changes that would have made the school more "competitive." On paper, their proposals made sense. But the principal stood firm because these changes would have contradicted the school's core values of inclusive education and character development. She didn't just defend these values, she took the time to explain why they mattered, how they shaped the school's approach, and what that meant for every student's future.

That's vision in action—not just having values but being able to articulate them clearly and connect them to concrete decisions and outcomes. It's about being able to say "no" to things that might look good on the surface but don't align with your core principles.

I've seen too many leaders try to skip this foundational work. They want to jump straight to strategy and tactics without doing the soul-searching required to develop a clear vision. It's like trying to navigate without a compass—you might move fast, but you're likely heading in the wrong direction.

Leading with Vision: Different Styles, Same True North

Here's something they don't teach you in leadership courses: There is no one-size-fits-all approach to bringing a vision to life. I learned this lesson by watching two very different leaders achieve remarkable results in their unique ways.

One boss wore suits that never quite fit right; his hair was always slightly disheveled. But when he opened his mouth, brilliant insights poured out. He was all substance, no flash. Another leader looked like they'd stepped out of a leadership manual: perfect appearance, polished presence. Both were effective, but for entirely different reasons.

This diversity in leadership styles isn't new. Again, Mahatma Gandhi and Nelson Mandela approached their visions of freedom and equality differently. Gandhi, with his quiet determination and simple living, made his very lifestyle a message. Mandela, on the other hand, learned to navigate both township streets and presidential palaces with equal grace. Different styles, yet the same unwavering commitment to their vision.

The key isn't finding the "right" style, it's finding the authentic one. The one that aligns with your values and resonates with your people. Let me break down what I've seen work, because at the end of the day, vision isn't about being impressive, it's about being understood. And understood vision becomes shared action.

Democratic Leadership: The Power of Collective Vision

When you invite team members to co-create rather than simply follow, the dynamic transforms entirely. During a critical planning phase for a major organizational initiative, I watched skeptical faces turn to engaged collaborators as we opened the floor for their insights. People who had never spoken up in meetings began offering innovative solutions to problems we hadn't even yet identified. The final blueprint wasn't just more comprehensive; it had champions at every level who felt personal ownership in seeing it succeed. This wasn't about relinquishing control but about multiplying commitment.

Transformational Leadership: Inspiring Change

This style is about painting a picture of what's possible and inspiring people to reach for it. Think of Frances Perkins from earlier in the book. She didn't just manage labor policies; she transformed how America thought about workers' rights. She took her personal experience of witnessing tragedy and turned it into a vision that changed millions of lives.

Servant Leadership: Leading from Behind

Sometimes, the most powerful vision is one that puts others first. When I work with young leaders, I tell them this story: Abraham Lincoln used to spend hours in telegraph offices during the Civil War, not just receiving updates but talking with ordinary soldiers and citizens. He understood that his vision for the nation had to be grounded in the real experiences of his people.

Harriet Tubman had no rank, no uniform, and no formal authority. She wasn't a general or a president. Yet her leadership changed lives and altered history. Through the Underground Railroad, she led over 70 enslaved people to freedom, risking her life again and again without ever holding a title. Her influence came from courage, consistency, and an unwavering moral compass.

Tubman didn't demand trust—she earned it. Those who followed her did so because she was someone they believed in. Her story reminds us that influence isn't about what's on your collar or your business card. It's about what you're willing to risk for others. That's the ripple effect at its most powerful: influence born of purpose, not position.

Situational Leadership: Adapting Without Compromising

Here's a truth I've learned: Your leadership style might need to change based on circumstances, but your vision shouldn't. I remember a crisis situation where I had to switch from a collaborative leader to a decisive leader in an instant. The style changed, but the underlying vision—taking care of our people while accomplishing the mission—remained constant.

Leadership styles must be authentic. I've watched leaders try to adopt styles that didn't fit their personality or values. It's like wearing someone else's shoes—you might be able to walk in them, but you'll never run at full speed.

This brings me to something crucial about vision and leadership style: The best leaders I've known have learned to adapt their approach without compromising their core vision. They're like skilled musicians who can play different genres while maintaining their signature sound.

No matter the tempo or terrain, the best leaders keep the tune of their vision recognizable. They don't compromise the message, they adjust the delivery.

Translating Vision into Reality: The Art of Clear Communication

Early in my career, I used to overcomplicate everything. I thought complexity made me sound smarter, more leader-like. Then one day, a mentor pulled me aside and said something I'll never forget: "If you can't explain your vision to a five-year-old, you don't understand it well enough yourself."

That hit me hard. That's why now, when I'm preparing to speak at places like the University of North Carolina Wilmington, I focus on three key themes. Just three. Not thirty. Not even ten. Three points that anyone can grasp, remember, and act on. This isn't about dumbing things down, it's about distilling wisdom to its essence.

This isn't simplicity for simplicity's sake—it's leadership discipline. If your vision can't survive a two-minute elevator ride or a 30-second combat update, it's not ready for the real world.

Think about how Lincoln delivered the *Gettysburg Address*. He didn't give a lengthy dissertation on constitutional law or military strategy. In just ten sentences, he redefined the entire purpose of the Civil War for the American people. That's the power of clear, focused communication.

When your people can repeat the vision in their own words and believe they have a role in making it real—that's when you've crossed from communication into conviction.

Here's my approach to communicating vision effectively:

1. Start with Why

Before I share any vision, I ask myself: "Why should my people care about this?" Frances Perkins didn't lead with statistics or regulations. She started with stories of real workers, real tragedies, and real needs. That's what made her vision for labor reform resonate across all levels of society. Context is critical.

2. Make It Personal

When I'm talking about cybersecurity or defense strategies, I always include examples that connect to everyday life. People need to see themselves in your vision. They need to understand how it affects them, their families, and their future.

3. Create Context

Context isn't just background information, it's the bridge between where you are and where you want to go. I learned this lesson the hard way when I saw leaders talk about technical specifications while their audience checked out mentally. Now I always ask myself: "Does this make sense to everyone in the room, and not just the experts?"

My friend Eric, a Marine I went through Intel school with, is another example of this done right. He served over eight years, earned his MBA at night school, and went on to find incredible success in the private sector. But here's what stands out most: he's not just focused and hard-working, he's an elite-level listener.

You notice it when you're playing a quiet round of golf with him. He doesn't waste time on surface talk. He asks thoughtful questions, the kind that actually matter. And then he listens—*really* listens. Because of that, he knows his people. He understands what drives them, where they struggle, and what they need to succeed. That's why his teams perform. Not because he micromanages, but because his vision includes understanding the humans behind the business.

Eric's not flashy. He's focused. And in leadership, that kind of listening builds trust faster than any strategy deck ever will.

Eric reminded me that your vision doesn't just live in PowerPoints or plans. It lives in the quality of the conversations you have every day. People follow leaders who see them.

4. Build in Milestones

Big visions can be overwhelming. That's why I break them down into achievable milestones. When we were implementing major changes in our command structure, we created what I called "victory markers"—small wins that showed we were moving in the right direction.

Recently, I worked with a team that was resistant to a new training initiative. Instead of forcing it through with authority, I took time to share stories about how similar training had saved lives in combat situations. Suddenly, what looked like just another requirement became part of a larger vision of excellence and readiness.

It's not just about being clear. It's about being consistent. Your informal conversations should reflect the same vision as your formal presentations. Your small decisions should align with your big announcements. Remember what I always tell my daughters: "The audio has to match the video."

Vision Checkpoints: Are You Leading with Clarity?

If you're not sure whether your vision is landing, ask yourself:

- Can my team explain our vision without reading a memo?

- Does every major decision trace back to a clear principle?

- Do I hear our vision echoed in meetings, plans, and hallway conversations?

- This month, have I personally told the story of *why* our vision matters?

A powerful vision isn't just understood; it's repeated, shared, and lived.

The Evolution of Vision: Staying True While Moving Forward

When I first took on leadership positions in the Marine Corps, I thought vision was something you set once and stuck to forever. Time and experience taught me otherwise. The core of your vision—your fundamental values and principles—those should be as solid as bedrock. But how you implement that vision needs to be as adaptable as water. We often say the enemy gets a vote, and I would add, so does Mother Nature.

Let me take you inside a moment that changed my perspective completely. I was the intelligence chief at Camp Lejeune, wearing my Master Gunnery Sergeant E9 rank that I'd earned through years of service. We were facing a critical decision about technology implementation that would affect how we gathered and processed intelligence. The "traditional" vision would have been to stick with proven methods. But I saw something most others didn't—a future where our enemies would use technology in ways we hadn't even imagined yet.

This wasn't just about updating equipment. It was about fundamentally rethinking how we operated. The challenge wasn't technical, it was human. How do you evolve a vision while keeping your team's trust? How do you move forward without losing sight of your core principles?

Look at the retail landscape. Circuit City stuck rigidly to its original vision of electronics retail. Best Buy, on the other hand, evolved its vision while maintaining its core purpose of serving customers. Circuit City is gone. Best Buy thrived. The difference? One saw its vision as a fixed destination; the other saw it as a living roadmap. The same could be said for Blockbuster, who missed seeing the cues for the digital revolution while Netflix didn't. We know how that story ended.

Reading the Horizon

Vision isn't just about where you are, it's about where the world is going. I make it a point to study trends daily, not just in defense or intelligence, but across business, technology, education, and culture. If I see something in the civilian world, or across our global competitors, that could give us an edge, I don't wait for it to be popular or proven. I start planning how to apply it.

I saw this firsthand while serving as the Command Senior Enlisted Leader at the Defense Intelligence Agency, U.S. Cyber Command, the National Security Agency, and U.S. Space Command. From that vantage point, it became clear: Future conflict isn't limited to land, air, and sea. It's already moving aggressively into new warfighting domains—**space and cyberspace.** That's where our adversaries are focusing their efforts. Not because they can't compete with tanks or aircraft carriers, but because they know our true advantage lies in our ability to sense, communicate, move, and strike faster than anyone else. They want to degrade what makes us a superior force, and they're using every tool they can to do it.

I watched our adversaries increase their use of drones on land, in the air, and at sea, and begin integrating AI to speed up their decision cycles. Meanwhile, here at home, I still heard some voices insisting the real fight would remain conventional. But I already knew the next battle would be fought in code, in orbit, and in milliseconds.

Wayne Gretzky said it best: "I skate to where the puck is going to be, not where it has been." That's what vision requires—not reacting to threats once they've arrived but anticipating them while others are still debating their existence.

Leadership isn't just about navigating the storm. It's about spotting the clouds before anyone else and setting a course that keeps your people ahead of the weather.

But here's the crucial part that most leadership books miss: Evolution isn't about chasing every new trend, it's about thoughtful, purposeful adaptation.

Building Resilient Vision

Your vision needs to be strong enough to withstand shocks but flexible enough to adapt to new realities. Think about Frances Perkins again. Her core vision of worker protection never wavered, but her methods evolved as she gained more political influence and understanding.

Creating Learning Organizations

I've learned to build feedback loops into every level of operation. We don't just assess results; we assess the vision itself. Is it still serving our purpose? Is it still inspiring our people? Is it still relevant to our changing world?

Here's a personal example that illustrates this point. Recently, I was consulting with a company that prided itself on "traditional" leadership values. Good values, time-tested approaches. But they were losing young talent left and right. Their vision hadn't evolved to address the needs and aspirations of a new generation of workers.

It wasn't just a retention issue, it was a relevance issue. Their vision hadn't aged well. And when your vision doesn't evolve, your best people outgrow it. Too often, leaders focus on talent management when they should be doubling down on talent utilization.

I shared with them a lesson I learned from studying Lincoln's presidency. During the Civil War, Lincoln's fundamental vision of preserving the Union never changed. But his understanding of what that meant evolved dramatically. He grew from seeing it as a purely political union to understanding it as a moral and human one. His vision didn't change, it deepened.

This brings me to something crucial about vision evolution: It's not just about adapting to external changes. It's about growing in your understanding of what your vision truly means. I've seen this in my own leadership journey. This comes from knowledge, like one gets from reading a book, as well as experience. Together, they equal wisdom.

When I first started leading teams, my vision was primarily about achieving objectives. Over time, it evolved to include developing people, building lasting capabilities, and creating environments where innovation could thrive. The core values of excellence, integrity, and service never changed. But my understanding of how to live those values grew richer and more nuanced.

The Technology Challenge

In today's rapidly evolving technological landscape, vision adaptation is more critical than ever. I see leaders struggling with this constantly. They either resist all change, clinging to "the way we've always done it," or chase every new trend without considering if it serves their core purpose.

The key is finding the sweet spot between stability and innovation. Your vision should be like a tree—roots planted firmly in your values, but branches reaching toward new opportunities and possibilities.

The Human Element

As your vision evolves, you must bring your people along with you. This means:

- Regular communication about why changes are necessary
- Honest discussions about challenges and opportunities
- Active involvement of team members in shaping the evolution
- Consistent reinforcement of core values while embracing new methods

The most successful vision adaptations I've seen weren't top-down mandates. They were collaborative evolutions where everyone felt invested in the outcome.

Measuring Progress While Staying Flexible

One of the trickiest aspects of evolving vision is knowing when you're on the right track. I've developed what I call "floating benchmarks"—progress markers that can adjust as circumstances change while still maintaining forward momentum.

Think of it like navigation at sea. Your destination (your core vision) might be fixed, but your route needs to adapt to weather, currents, and conditions. Success isn't just reaching the destination; it's reaching it safely with your crew intact and stronger for the journey.

And leadership is the vessel. Weak leadership cracks under pressure. Strong leadership—anchored in values, guided by vision—adjusts course without losing direction.

Looking Ahead: The Ripple Effect

Vision is your invitation to others. It's how you get people to row in the same direction even when the waves get high. Get it wrong, and your team will drift. Get it right, and they'll move with purpose, even when you're not in the boat.

In the next chapter, we'll explore how true leadership influence extends far beyond formal authority. You'll learn how small actions create lasting ripples, why character matters more than rank or titles, and how to build the kind of influence that continues long after you've left the room. Because here's the truth about leadership: Your most significant impact often comes from moments when you're not even trying to lead. Long after the title fades, the ripple of who you were will still move others forward.

CHAPTER TAKEAWAYS

Vision Requires Clarity and Context. Your vision must be understandable at every level of your organization. If people can't see themselves in your vision, they won't invest in making it reality.

Build Vision on Core Values. Let your principles guide strategic decisions, and demonstrate those principles through consistent actions. Values aren't just words on a wall; they're your framework for making tough calls when stakes are high.

Adapt Style While Maintaining Vision. Modify your approach based on situation and team needs but keep your core mission constant. Authentic leadership means finding your own way to communicate and execute vision effectively.

Create Sustainable Impact. Success isn't just about achieving immediate goals. It's about building systems and developing people who continue to grow after you're gone. Your vision should outlast your leadership.

Future-Proof Your Vision. Stay ahead of changes in your industry while building resilience into your organizational culture. A strong vision flexes with new challenges without breaking under pressure.

Remember: Leadership vision isn't just about destination, it's about transformation. Make it clear enough to follow, bold enough to inspire, and flexible enough to evolve. In the next chapter, we'll explore how to extend your influence beyond formal authority—because true leadership isn't about rank or position, it's about impact.

*"The greatest leader is not necessarily the one
who does the greatest things.
He is the one that gets people to do the greatest things."*
— *Ronald Reagan*

— 7 —

THE RIPPLE EFFECT:
INFLUENCE BEYOND AUTHORITY

Recently, two conversations reminded me of why influence matters more than authority. A Marine reached out about a discussion we'd had in Monterey back in 2017, a conversation I barely remembered. Later that same day, a former private, now a senior leader herself, contacted me about a brief interaction that had shaped her career path. These weren't dramatic moments. No orders were given. No authority was exercised. Just genuine conversations where I took time to listen and share what I'd learned.

These moments happen every day in leadership, but we often miss their significance. We're so focused on formal authority—the rank, the title, the position—that we overlook the quiet power of genuine influence. It's like throwing a stone into a pond. The initial splash might seem small, but the ripples keep expanding, touching shores you can't even see.

Think about Benjamin Franklin arriving in Paris in 1776. He had no formal diplomatic training, no official government position at first, and was representing a nation that barely existed.[17] Yet he became one of the most influential figures in French society and ultimately secured crucial support for American independence.[18] How? Not through authority, because he had none. He did it through building relationships, demonstrating integrity, and showing genuine interest in French culture and ideas.

Franklin understood that influence came through connection rather than position. He spent countless hours in French salons and scientific societies, engaging with both intellectuals and ordinary citizens.[19] Rather than pushing American interests aggressively, he took time to understand French customs and cultural sensitivities.[4] He even dressed simply, wearing neither a wig nor a sword, playing into French fantasies about American authenticity and simplicity.[20]

What's remarkable about Franklin's approach was his patient building of influence. While other American envoys demanded immediate action, Franklin cultivated relationships, hosted dinners, and engaged in scientific discussions that seemed far removed from diplomatic matters. He understood something fundamental about influence: it grows through genuine connection and consistent demonstration of character, not through positional authority.

The results speak for themselves. By the time France committed to supporting American independence, Franklin had built such strong networks of influence that he could accomplish in hours what might have taken others months of going through formal diplomatic channels.[21]

This is what real influence looks like in practice. It's not about forcing compliance through position or power. It's about building trust through consistent actions, demonstrating genuine care for others' success, and maintaining unwavering integrity in all situations.

Building Influence Through Integrity

General Joe Dunford perfectly illustrates this principle. After serving as chairman of the Joint Chiefs of Staff under both President Obama and President Trump—two administrations with vastly different approaches and priorities—Dunford has maintained absolute discretion about his private counsel to both presidents. He's been offered millions to write tell-all books. Publishers have promised bestseller status. Media outlets have pressured him to weigh in on political controversies.

But Dunford understands something fundamental about influence: it iss built through consistency and integrity, not through exploiting past positions for personal gain. By maintaining his principles, he's preserved his ability to influence future generations of military leaders. They know they can trust him because he's demonstrated, through actions rather than words, that some principles matter more than personal profit or public attention.

Eleanor Roosevelt's influence went far beyond her role as First Lady. When appointed to the UN Human Rights Commission in 1947, she had no formal diplomatic authority.[22] Yet she became the driving force behind the Universal Declaration of Human Rights, working across deep ideological divides during the early Cold War.[23] She spent hours studying complex diplomatic papers, meeting with representatives from opposing nations, and building consensus through patient relationship-building rather than authority.[24]

When Soviet representatives tried to block progress, she didn't rely on American power; she invited them to tea, listened to their concerns, and found ways to address their underlying issues while maintaining the declaration's core principles.[25] During one particularly tense negotiation, she defused a potential walkout by sharing personal stories about her own struggles with human rights issues in America, demonstrating that self-reflection and honesty build more influence than defensive posturing.[26]

Roosevelt's approach to building influence went beyond traditional diplomacy. She wrote a daily newspaper column called "My Day," reaching millions of ordinary citizens with complex international issues explained in simple, relatable terms.[27] When faced with segregation at speaking events, she would quietly rearrange the seating, demonstrating through actions rather than arguments how to effect change.[28]

Her influence continued to grow even after leaving official positions. By consistently demonstrating her commitment to human rights through concrete actions rather than mere rhetoric, she built a network of trust that transcended political divisions.[29] Her work with the American Association for the United Nations showed how private citizens could influence international policy through persistent, principled advocacy.[30]

I see too many leaders today trying to work this equation backwards. They think the position will automatically grant them influence. But it doesn't work that way. I've known plenty of high-ranking officials who couldn't influence anyone beyond their direct chain of command. I've also known junior enlisted personnel and civilians who could shape entire organizations through their example and earned trust.

The Power of Positive Actions

Every action you take as a leader creates ripples, but here's what most leadership books won't tell you: The smallest actions often create the biggest waves. I've been invited to speak at several Marine Corps Balls this year, not because of my former rank but because of hundreds of small interactions that built trust over time. This led to a majority of the Marines in one specific unit voting for me to be their guest of honor, whereas a more senior general officer would traditionally be the one at the mic.

Real influence is not about grand gestures or formal authority. It's about consistently demonstrating through actions that you care about people's success, that you're willing to invest time in their development, and that you'll stand by your principles even when it's inconvenient.

Think about two radically different approaches to influence that emerged in post-war America. In 1947, Secretary of State George Marshall proposed a plan to rebuild war-torn Europe, including former enemy nations.[31] Around the same time, Senator Joseph McCarthy began wielding influence through fear, destroying American careers and lives with often-baseless accusations of communist sympathy.[32]

The contrast in these approaches teaches us something profound about influence versus authority. Marshall understood that real influence comes through support, cooperation, and mutual respect. Instead of punishing defeated nations, he proposed helping them rebuild.[33] Rather than dictating terms from Washington, he involved European nations in designing their own recovery, creating buy-in that no amount of authority could have achieved.[34]

Meanwhile, McCarthy chose the path of authority without legitimate influence. He used his senatorial position to conduct witch hunts that ruined countless lives through baseless accusations and character assassination.[35] While he temporarily gained power through fear, his influence evaporated once people stood up to his bullying tactics. Today, "McCarthyism" is synonymous with the abuse of authority, while the Marshall Plan is studied as a model of positive influence.[36]

The results speak for themselves. The Marshall Plan helped create lasting alliances that have endured for over 70 years.[37] McCarthy's influence, built on fear rather than trust, collapsed completely within just a few years.[38] One man chose to build influence through positive action; the other tried to maintain power through fear and intimidation. One is remembered as a statesman, and the other as a cautionary tale.

Modern leaders can learn crucial lessons from Marshall's approach. When I worked with intelligence units transitioning to new systems, I used this same principle. Instead of mandating changes from above, we brought in operators from every level to help design the implementation. Just like Marshall understood that French industrial workers knew better than Washington bureaucrats what their factories needed, I knew that our front-line analysts often had better insights than senior leadership about what tools would work best.

I saw this principle work dramatically when helping a struggling unit improve its performance metrics. Instead of issuing directives, we gathered input from every level—from junior analysts to senior staff. The solutions they developed weren't just good, they were better than anything leadership alone would have created. More importantly, because people felt ownership of these solutions they committed to making them work.

This brings me to a crucial point about influence: it multiplies through others. Marshall didn't just rebuild Europe; he created a model for international cooperation that influenced decades of diplomacy. Similarly, when we build influence through positive actions and inclusive leadership, we create ripple effects that extend far beyond our immediate sphere.

The Power of Trust and Professional Reputation

Trust-based influence doesn't happen by accident. It's built through thousands of small decisions to do the right thing, especially when it's difficult. Take my current role as a consultant. I work with a company that doesn't pay top dollar, but I stay because the CEO exemplifies the kind of leadership that creates genuine influence. He mentors, molds, advises, and leads with authenticity. He's consistent, balanced, and measured in everything he does. Everyone who works there would do anything for him, not because they have to, but because they want to.

This brings me to a crucial point about professional reputation. In today's world, with social media and instant communication, it's easy to think influence comes from visibility or "personal branding." But real influence, the kind that lasts, comes from consistent actions that demonstrate character. I've seen this play out repeatedly with leaders who focused on short-term visibility rather than long-term credibility. It's like the difference between being classic and being trendy. Classic wins the day in the long run.

Consider this reality check: When a CEO steps down or a commander moves on, you can immediately tell the depth of their influence by how people talk about them when they're gone. Are they remembered for their title, or for their impact on people's lives? Are they missed because of their authority, or because of their influence? The old adage, 'People may not remember what you said, but they will remember how you made them feel,' applies here.

Some of the most powerful examples of influence derive from how you handle adversity. A few years ago, I worked with a senior enlisted leader who took over a unit suffering from low morale and a profound lack of trust. She didn't walk in barking orders or throwing her weight around. Instead, she quietly watched, listened more than she spoke, and started making small but powerful changes— reorganizing the duty schedule to give overworked team members time to reset, getting involved during tough missions, and supporting her team when they needed it most.

Within six months, the entire tone of the unit had shifted. Performance improved. Retention stabilized. And trust was restored—not because of her title, but because of how she showed up every day. She didn't demand respect—she earned it.

The truth about influence is this: if you have to remind people of your authority, you've already lost your influence. I learned this lesson watching great leaders who never had to mention their rank; their influence came from who they were, not what position they held.

Creating Lasting Legacy Through Informal Influence

The most powerful kind of influence outlasts your presence. Here's a reality I learned when transitioning out of active service: When you rely solely on positional authority, your impact ends the moment you leave. But when you've built genuine influence, it continues to ripple outward. A simple way to measure this is whether or not you're invited back once you leave—if they still call you, or if they quickly take down your photo and move on. Your rank, title, and position may have put you at the table, but your genuine love for your people and your support for them is what earns you influence.

General Dunford exemplifies this principle perfectly. Think about the pressure he faces daily: political operatives, media outlets, and publishers, all offering millions for his insider perspective on two very different presidencies. But he understands something profound about lasting influence: it comes from maintaining your principles, not exploiting your positions. By refusing to politicize his service or break confidence, he's preserved something more valuable than any book advance—his ability to influence future generations of military leaders. The General maintains his moral compass despite the option to exploit a relationship and make millions. This timeless and classic approach makes him one of the most trusted leaders of our generation.

This isn't just about high-level leadership. I see this play out every day in more immediate ways. Just recently, I consulted with a small veteran-owned business. The CEO runs an organization where everyone genuinely wants to be there, despite being able to earn more elsewhere. Why? Because he's mastered the art of influence through authentic leadership. His team members don't just work for him, they grow with him.

After retirement, many leaders make the mistake of clinging to their former titles, trying to maintain authority they no longer possess. Now that I'm retired, some of the Marines who once worked for me have become my colleagues, my business partners, even my mentors. I used to give them direction. Now I ask them for advice. Watching them thrive is one of the greatest joys of my post-military life.

This is what I mean when I say people will follow rank because they have to, but if you lead with character, connection, and consistency, they'll follow you because they want to. That kind of influence doesn't retire when your title does. It gets stronger.

True influence also means being willing to be influenced in return. I've learned as much from my former Marines as I ever taught them. When I reach out for advice today, it's not a formality, it's because I genuinely value their perspective. Leadership isn't a one-way street. When you lead with humility, you open yourself to insights that sharpen your own impact.

I've taken a different approach than most to my transition from military service to the "real world." I focus on being just Scott. I like to tell people that I leased my rank; it brought me an earned title and position, but once I retired, I had to return it and go back to just being Scott. That transition is critical but hard for many to do. Holding on to the past not only holds you back but also limits your opportunities and keeps you stuck celebrating old wins rather than seeking new ones. Yes, some people still use my rank out of professional courtesy, but true influence doesn't come from what people call you. It comes from how you impact their lives.

Your title may open the door, but it's your testimony that keeps it open.

I've seen leaders introduce themselves with a mouthful of accomplishments, and lose the room in seconds. Others walk in quietly, and everyone listens. Why? Because one demands attention while the other has already earned it. Your legacy isn't what's on your nameplate; it's what people say about you when you're not in the room.

For instance, I recently got a call from someone I'd advised years ago. They weren't calling the retired Master Gunnery Sergeant; they were calling someone who had taken the time to explain not just what to do, but why it mattered. This type of conversation started left of the conversation itself years prior. These phone calls don't happen unless all of those things happen prior. That's the kind of influence that sustains itself.

This approach to building lasting influence requires a fundamental shift in how we think about leadership. It's not about the positions we hold or the authority we wield but about the lives we touch and the ripples we create. Consider how Eleanor Roosevelt's influence continued long after her official role as First Lady ended. She had built such strong networks of trust and demonstrated such consistent commitment to her values that she remained a powerful voice for human rights until her death.

The key to creating this kind of lasting impact lies in how you treat people when you don't need anything from them. It's about building relationships before you need them, maintaining connections without an agenda, and always being ready to offer help without expecting immediate return.

Building and Maintaining Influence in Practice

The true test of influence is what happens in the quiet moments, not the dramatic ones. It's in the daily decisions that seem insignificant at the time: choosing to stay late to help a junior team member understand a process, taking time to explain the 'why' behind a decision, or simply demonstrating genuine interest in someone's development when there's nothing in it for you.

This illustrates a crucial point about lasting influence: it's built in the margins, in the moments when no one's watching. Too many leaders save their best efforts for the spotlight moments, polishing their performance for evaluations or big presentations. But real influence grows in everyday interactions, the consistent demonstrations of character and care when there's no audience and no immediate reward.

Think about how this plays out in today's organizations. I'm seeing more virtual teams, more remote work, more technology-mediated interactions. Some leaders see this as a barrier to building influence. But I've found it creates new opportunities for meaningful connection. When you reach out to check on someone's family or remember details from your last conversation, it means even more because it shows intentional effort to maintain a connection across distance. Where others may comment on a social media post, you call them on the phone; when others send an email, you send a handwritten letter; when others want to do a virtual cup of coffee, you schedule time to see them in person. Going the extra mile is not just noticed, it's felt forever. If you want to become the leader you're meant to be, you must do more than the average leaders have done for you.

Here's what I've learned about maintaining influence in our modern environment:

- Stay connected without agenda—reach out when you don't need anything
- Keep investing in others' success even after your paths diverge
- Maintain your principles consistently, especially when it costs you something
- Focus on adding value rather than asserting authority

Influence isn't free; it comes with a cost. You'll invest more time, more energy, and more emotional labor than most people are willing to give. You'll pour into others with no guarantee of return. But here's the tradeoff: you build something that outlives you. Something that matters.

Influence demands that you show up even when you're tired. That you make the extra call, send the extra message, remember the name no one else does. Most of the world settles for being liked or feared. But influence? Influence is earned by doing the work no one sees, with consistency no one requires, and with heart no one can fake.

The most powerful example of this approach comes from watching how influence compounds over time. When my mentees become mentors themselves, when they pass along not just information but approaches and values—that's when I see the true ripple effect of influence-based leadership.

Here's the challenge I leave you with: Start tracking your influence the way most people track authority. Not in promotions, awards, or likes, but in lives impacted, doors opened for others, and people who reach out years later to say, "You helped me see what was possible." That's how you know your influence mattered. That's when the ripple becomes a wave.

The legacy of influence isn't measured by how many people worked for you. It's measured by how many leaders you helped develop. Lasting influence is never about how loudly you spoke, but about how deeply you listened, how much you gave, and how many others you equipped to carry the mission forward.

CHAPTER TAKEAWAYS

- **True Influence Outlasts Authority.** Build relationships before you need them and focus on character over position power. The moment you leave a position, your authority ends, but genuine influence continues shaping decisions and careers long after you're gone.

- **Actions Create Ripples.** Small interactions can have major long-term impact, so pay attention to informal moments. Like throwing a stone in a pond, you often can't see where your influence will reach or how it might shape someone's future decisions.

- **Trust Is the Foundation.** Maintain your principles even when it costs you something, and let results speak louder than titles. Trust isn't built in crisis moments; it's accumulated through countless small decisions to do the right thing, especially when it's difficult.

- **Create Lasting Impact.** Focus on developing others and sharing knowledge and context, not just directions. Your greatest legacy won't be the decisions you made, but the leaders you helped develop who will make decisions long after you're gone.

- **Stay Authentic.** Don't cling to past titles or try to maintain authority you no longer possess. True influence comes from who you are and how you affect others, not from position or power. The most powerful form of influence is being consistently yourself.

In the next chapter, we'll explore how to maintain resilience through the challenges of leadership, because influence without endurance isn't enough.

Influence Audit – Ask Yourself:

- Whom did I mentor this month?
- Whom do I check on without needing anything in return?
- Did I uphold my values when no one was watching?
- To whom have I reached back in order to help up the ladder?
- Would they follow me now, even if I had no title?

Don't ask who reports to you. Ask who listens to you when they don't have to, and why. That's where real influence lives.

"You can't go out and practice average Monday through Friday, then expect to play great on Sunday."
— *Tom Brady*

— 8 —

RESILIENCE IN RANK: OVERCOMING OBSTACLES ON YOUR LEADERSHIP JOURNEY

I've kidnapped people before—four Marines, to be precise.

Before you start questioning your choice in leadership books, let me assure you it was more of an "unauthorized personnel acquisition" than a federal offense. It happened back in 2002-2003 while I was stationed at the sun-scorched purgatory known as Twenty-Nine Palms, California. For the uninitiated, being stationed at Twenty-Nine Palms is not an assignment most people fight over. It's a slice of desert north of San Diego that makes Death Valley look like a luxury resort. The Marines who end up there generally aren't there by choice. Married? Your spouse will wonder what war crime you committed to deserve this posting. Single? Let's just say the local wildlife outnumbers dating prospects about ten thousand to one.

As the Iraq War loomed on the horizon, we were deployed to Kuwait. My Regiment, 7th Marines—the folks who would actually be in the line of fire—operated with a skeleton crew. Meanwhile, Division Headquarters was bursting at the seams with personnel. I remember driving to a meeting at the 1st Marine Division G2 (that's "intelligence section" for those of you who speak civilian) and finding the combat operations center so overstaffed I couldn't even squeeze through the door. It was like watching someone hoard resources for a hurricane that was going to hit someone else's house.

As I walked away, seething with frustration, I spotted four fresh-faced Marines sitting outside. They had that "just graduated from intelligence school" look—equal parts eager and terrified, their uniforms still creased in all the right places. I approached them casually.

"What are you Marines doing?" I asked.

"Waiting to check in, Gunnery Sergeant," one replied, as they all stood up and responded. "Just finished intel school."

In that moment, I made a decision that definitely wasn't in any leadership manual. I straightened up and used my most official voice: "I'm here to pick you up. Get in the vehicle."

Did headquarters send me to collect these Marines? Absolutely not. Did I have any authority whatsoever to commandeer personnel? Negative. But sometimes leadership requires a creative redistribution of resources.

I drove them back to my headquarters like contraband, then pulled my Major aside and said, "Sir, I've acquired four intelligence specialists. If anyone asks, we've never seen them before in our lives."

What followed was the real test. We deployed with our "borrowed" Marines and crossed the line of departure into Iraq. We fought through dust storms and firefights, all the way to Baghdad. Those four Marines became integral to our operations; it turns out they were exactly where they needed to be.

Months later, the bureaucratic gears finally turned enough for someone at Headquarters Marine Corps to notice the discrepancy. I received a call: "Gunnery Sergeant Stalker, do you happen to know the whereabouts of four Marines who were supposed to report to Division?"

I didn't hesitate. "Yes, sir. I took them."

Then I explained why—how Division was overstaffed while we were undermanned; how these Marines had provided critical intelligence support during combat operations; how two of them had even volunteered to extend their deployments and remain in Iraq with me while our unit, 7th Marines, rotated home.

Instead of the court-martial I half-expected, Headquarters simply adjusted the paperwork and officially reassigned them to us.

This wasn't leadership by the book. It was leadership by necessity. In the field, resilience isn't about following proper channels; it's about identifying what needs to be done and having the courage to do it, even when it means bending a few rules and accepting potential consequences. Because oftentimes, it's not about what you did, it's about what you got done.

Would I recommend kidnapping personnel as a standard management practice? Probably not. But I would recommend developing the judgment to know when the mission demands unorthodox solutions, and the backbone to stand by those decisions when the inevitable questions come.

That kind of decision-making—bold, imperfect, and high-risk—

is what separates checkbox leaders from battlefield leaders. It's easy to lead when everything fits inside a PowerPoint slide. It's much harder when the stakes are real and you've got seconds to act. That's where resilience kicks in—not just physically, but morally and mentally. Which brings me to one of history's most resilient commanders.

Admiral Yi Sun-sin

Admiral Yi Sun-sin, the legendary 16th century Korean naval commander, provides a powerful example of overcoming seemingly insurmountable obstacles on the leadership journey.[39]

Despite facing political sabotage, imprisonment, demotion, and overwhelming military disadvantages, Yi never wavered in his commitment to his country.[40] What makes Yi's story particularly relevant to modern leadership challenges was his ability to maintain integrity while navigating a politically treacherous environment. When falsely accused by jealous rivals and stripped of his rank, Yi accepted his demotion with dignity rather than becoming bitter or abandoning his principles.[41] This demonstrates how true resilience isn't just about personal survival but maintaining your moral compass when facing adversity.

Yi's most famous achievement—defeating 133 Japanese ships with just 13 of his own using innovative "turtle ships" and superior tactical knowledge[42]—shows how resilience often requires creative thinking and making the absolute most of limited resources. For today's leaders facing resource constraints or seemingly impossible challenges, Yi's example reminds us that innovation combined with unwavering determination can overcome even the most daunting odds.[43]

Sometimes this means making difficult decisions that push boundaries. Throughout history, from Admiral Yi to modern military leaders, we see that occasionally the most resilient leaders must operate in gray areas when rigid systems fail to address urgent needs. The point isn't that we should all go around kidnapping personnel or defying authority. The point is that resilience in leadership often means having the courage to make tough calls when systems fail us, and the strength to handle whatever comes next.

That's what this chapter is about—building the kind of resilience that lets you weather storms, bounce back from setbacks, and keep pushing forward when everything in you wants to quit. Because it's not the strongest leaders who succeed in the long run. It's the most resilient ones.

The Gift of Stress: Building Mental Toughness

Here's something that might sound crazy at first: Stress is a gift. This concept can be illustrated by looking at the sport of powerlifting.

When you're training with weights, the only way to get stronger is to deliberately add stress to your muscles. Add five pounds here and an extra rep there. Without that stress, there's no growth. No adaptation. No improvement. The same principle applies to leadership.

That kind of pressure—repeated, increasing, and sometimes uncomfortable—is exactly what forged my leadership over three decades in uniform. But growth through stress doesn't always look like triumph. Sometimes it looks like rejection, resistance, or being told you don't fit the mold. I've lived all of that. And one of the clearest examples came not during combat or crisis—but the day before I retired.

I was standing in a mostly empty auditorium, running through the ceremony rehearsal with my Commander and the Protocol Chief—two people I respect deeply. The Protocol Chief was in charge of the script, making sure every moment would run smoothly.

At one point in the run-through, she approached us with an update: the retirement medal I was scheduled to receive had just been downgraded by the Marine Corps. She asked what we wanted to do next.

Now, for most people, especially after a 31-year career, that might have been a gut punch. But for me? I barely blinked. I'd seen this before.

Earlier in my career, I was put in for an Air Medal. It got downgraded. Later, I was submitted for a Bronze Star. Same story. That's not me being bitter, that's just Marine Corps culture. Part of it is tradition, and part of it is the rigid mindset that certain awards are only appropriate at certain ranks, regardless of performance or impact. There's very little room for nuance or leadership that doesn't fit the mold.

And I never really fit the mold.

I wasn't a Sergeant Major. I was a Master Gunnery Sergeant. And in many ways, I was a square peg in a round-hole system. I operated in the gray while the institution preferred black-and-white. I had served as the first and only Marine Corps Senior Enlisted Leader for the Defense Intelligence Agency, then later for U.S. Cyber Command and the National Security Agency. I was retiring as the first and only Marine Corps Senior Enlisted Leader for U.S. Space Command.

But the system didn't know what to do with someone like me. One of the most senior Marines I ever served with once looked at me and said, "I have no idea what to do with you next." And he meant it as a compliment. I had outgrown the model. I had built something new.

So when the award was downgraded the day before my retirement, I wasn't surprised. What surprised me was how surprised they were. This was standard operating procedure. I even offered, again, to skip the medal presentation during the ceremony altogether—to just do it quietly, off-stage, if at all. But my Commander overruled me. He knew it wasn't about the medal—it was about what the moment represented to others.

So we went through with the ceremony. I received the medal. And the next day, life went on.

But the medal didn't define me then, and it doesn't define me now. All the awards I've earned are in a box in my attic. Someday, my daughters might pull them out, dust them off, and tell stories about their dad. And that's enough for me.

Adversity is real. But we get to define how we respond to it—and just as importantly, we get to decide who defines us.

—

That retirement ceremony marked the end of one chapter—but it wasn't the end of me. If anything, it forced me to redefine what strength really meant. I didn't just walk away from the uniform—I walked into a new challenge: rebuilding myself, physically and mentally, on my own terms. What started as a response to adversity became a new mission. And like every mission before, it required discipline, discomfort, and growth under pressure.

In less than five years, I went from considering retirement to setting personal records and making it into the Pentagon Powerlifting Hall of Fame. Through the stress I endured from the weight training program, I'm not only stronger, but I feel better than ever, and I have no issues with my back, even in my 50s.

Think about Ernest Shackleton during his ill-fated Antarctic expedition. When his ship Endurance was crushed by ice in 1914, he could have succumbed to despair. Instead, he used that immense stress as fuel for one of the most remarkable leadership achievements in history. He kept 27 men alive for nearly two years in the harshest conditions imaginable, leading them on a 720-nautical-mile journey in small boats across the stormy Southern Ocean.

This is what I mean about stress being a gift. Whether it's in business, military operations, or life in general, stress reveals our true capabilities. It forces us to adapt, innovate, and grow stronger. If you want to see a great leader, look for those who are calm in a crisis.

I see this play out in the business world all the time. Recently, I asked Josh, my friend who owns the fast-food chains, what keeps him up at night. His answer? "What if someone invents a pill that makes people not feel hungry anymore?" That's the kind of stress that makes you think strategically, that pushes you to innovate and adapt before you're forced to.

The key is understanding that resilience isn't about avoiding stress, it's about using it constructively. When you're leading one person, then a small team, then an entire organization, each level brings new stress. But if you see these challenges as opportunities for growth rather than obstacles to overcome, everything changes.

This is why I say drive is more important than grit. In this story we have someone who is planning ahead so he's able to overcome, and he's posturing himself to not only succeed but also be in the best position to weather the storm. Grit will get you through it, but if you're not forward-thinking and planning for the future, you will not be resilient.

There's a difference between the pressure you feel every day and the sudden crisis that hits out of nowhere. Daily pressure wears you down quietly, like water on rock. A sudden crisis is like a hammer. Resilient leaders prepare for both. They don't just strengthen themselves for the big moments; they build habits and systems that make them durable over the long haul. If you're only training for the sprint, you'll never finish the marathon.

Look at the sports world. I have a bit of a unique perspective on this as someone who's watched both sides of success. When you look at teams like the Washington Commanders (my wife's a big fan) versus the sustained success of teams like the New England Patriots, you see something interesting. Success can make you complacent. Sports fans often get comfortable with too much winning.

That's why I tell leaders this: Success is rented, and rent is due every day.

That's why resilience is about more than just bouncing back from failure. It's about maintaining your edge even when things are going well. As we say in the military, "The more you sweat in training, the less you bleed in combat." You must deliberately seek out stress, push your boundaries, test your limits.

The problem is that too many leaders try to avoid stress altogether. They stick to what's comfortable, what's known. But that's like trying to get stronger without ever adding weight to the bar. It just doesn't work.

Personal Oil Check: Foundation of Resilience

You know how your car has a dipstick to check the oil level? Well, I've learned that resilient leaders need their own version of a dipstick check—a way to monitor their fundamental systems before things go critically wrong.

Here's what I mean. Every day, I do a personal oil check on five key areas:

1. **Sleep:** Am I getting enough quality rest?

2. **Nutrition:** Am I fueling my body properly?

3. **Exercise:** Am I maintaining physical readiness?

4. **Mental engagement:** Am I learning and staying intellectually sharp?

5. **Human connection:** Am I maintaining relationships with people who matter?

When something's off in my life, it usually traces back to one of these areas being low. For instance, I might find myself having a few too many cocktails, which affects my sleep, which then impacts my physical fitness. Add in some travel that disrupts my routine, and suddenly my whole system is out of balance.

General Matthew Ridgway

General Matthew Ridgway exemplifies extraordinary resilience in modern military leadership, particularly during the Korean War. In December 1950, Ridgway took command of the demoralized Eighth

Army after its previous commander was killed in a jeep accident, inheriting a force in full retreat with catastrophically low morale. The situation appeared hopeless—Chinese forces had shattered UN lines, Seoul was about to fall, and many advocated complete withdrawal from the Korean peninsula.[44] Against this backdrop of apparent defeat, Ridgway demonstrated the essence of leadership resilience.

What distinguished Ridgway's approach was his immediate focus on restoring fighting spirit while implementing practical tactical reforms. Rather than accepting defeat, he personally visited frontline units, assessed battlefield conditions firsthand, and instituted his "stand or die" orders that halted the retreat.[45] Within weeks, Ridgway transformed a broken army into an effective fighting force that not only stopped the Chinese advance but eventually recaptured Seoul.

Like Admiral Yi, Ridgway's leadership demonstrated that resilience isn't merely about personal mental toughness, but about the capacity to inspire it in others when circumstances seem most dire. His leadership philosophy, which emphasized clarity of mission and personal example, offers a timeless model for leaders facing their own seemingly insurmountable challenges.[46]

Ridgway understood something fundamental about resilience: it requires having all necessary resources properly managed. While he restored tactical positioning and combat effectiveness, he simultaneously focused on logistics and supply lines, ensuring his troops had what they needed to sustain operations. This comprehensive approach to resource management highlights an often-overlooked aspect of leadership resilience.

Here's something most leadership books won't tell you: financial planning is also part of resilience. Even if you're making minimum wage, can you save one extra dollar a week? Building that financial cushion isn't just about money, it's about creating peace of mind that lets you focus on leadership rather than survival.

Let me ask you something: If you lost your primary income source today, how long could you sustain your responsibilities without panic? A week? A month? A year? That's not a scare tactic, it's a resilience metric. Start there. Build from it. Leadership begins with personal stability.

In our family, we have a saying: "You're allowed to have a bad day. You just can't be mean." Some mornings, one of us might wake up just not feeling it. Maybe it's my wife, maybe it's me, maybe it's one of our girls. We don't always need to know why; we just need to acknowledge it and give each other space. That's resilience at the family level.

But here's where a lot of leaders get it wrong—they think resilience means never showing weakness, never admitting struggle. That's not resilience, that's denial. Real resilience is about having systems in place to check your levels and address problems before they become crises.

Katharine Graham's journey offers a profound example of leadership resilience in the face of personal tragedy and professional skepticism. When her husband's suicide in 1963 suddenly thrust her into the role of publisher of *The Washington Post*, Graham, who had no formal business training and lived in an era of intense gender discrimination, inherited a struggling newspaper in a precarious financial position.[47] Industry insiders, board members, and even family friends doubted her capacity to lead, with many expecting her to serve as merely a figurehead while men made the actual decisions.

But resilience isn't just forged on the battlefield or in the board-room—it's forged in the fire of personal tragedy and professional doubt. There's no armor thick enough to stop life from hitting you. The question isn't whether it will; the question is who you become when it does.

What makes Graham's story particularly relevant to resilience in leadership is how she transformed from self-described "door-mat wife" to one of publishing's most formidable figures. Despite overwhelming self-doubt and external criticism, Graham gradually asserted control, making consequential decisions that ultimately defined her leadership legacy. Her unwavering resilience was most evident during the Pentagon Papers crisis and Watergate scandal, when she risked the Post's financial viability and her family's owner-ship by publishing stories that challenged the Nixon administration. [48]Like both Admiral Yi and General Ridgway, Graham demon-strated that authentic resilience involves making difficult decisions under extreme pressure while remaining true to core principles. Her transformation from reluctant inheritor to courageous publisher demonstrates how resilience often develops not before challenges arise, but through the process of confronting them.[49]

I've built resilience into my business planning too. I know I can probably do consulting work for another two to four years before I start becoming outdated. New people will come into the defense community who are more current, more relevant. That's just reality. So, I'm planning now for that transition, thinking five to ten years down the road, and taking on less consulting work to build for the future that I am anticipating.

This kind of systematic approach to resilience isn't glamorous. It's about daily habits, regular check-ins, and honest self-assessment. But it's what keeps you going when others falter. A bonus to this is when you have a friend or loved one who can tell you what you need to hear, not what you want to hear.

Think of it like preventive maintenance for your leadership capacity. Just like you wouldn't wait for your engine to seize before checking the oil, you shouldn't wait for a personal crisis before checking your fundamental systems.

During a recent stretch of speaking engagements, I found myself in three different time zones in five days. My normal routines were disrupted, my sleep was off, and I could feel my effectiveness starting to slip. That's when the personal dipstick check became crucial.

Instead of pushing through and pretending everything was fine (which is what many leaders do), I took stock:

Sleep: Below optimal level, needed adjustment

Nutrition: Slipping into too many "convenient" meals

Exercise: Missing regular workouts

Mental engagement: High from the speaking events

Human connection: Strong with audiences but missing family time

This assessment enabled me to make immediate corrections rather than waiting for a full breakdown. I adjusted my schedule to ensure seven hours of sleep, found a hotel gym, and scheduled specific times to FaceTime with my family.

Here's something else about resilience that might surprise you.

It's contagious. When your team sees you openly performing these self-checks and making adjustments, it gives them permission to do the same. It creates a culture of sustainable high performance rather than burnout. Even a machine can only redline for so long before it breaks.

When I talk about building financial resilience, I'm not just talking about saving money, though that's important. I'm talking about building a comprehensive approach to sustainability in your career and life. Ideally, this includes more than one stream of income and no single point of failure.

General Ridgway didn't just focus on military tactics; he understood that resilience required addressing fundamental needs first. He improved the soldiers' food, their equipment, and their rest periods. He recognized that an army, like any organization, can't be resilient if its basic systems are compromised.

The same principle applies in the business world. I know a restaurant owner who seems to handle every crisis—supply chain issues, staffing problems, economic downturns—with remarkable calm. His approach isn't magic, it's methodical. He cross-trains his staff, maintains strong relationships with multiple suppliers, and builds reserves during good times. It's all about creating systems that can weather storms.

Katherine Graham didn't just focus on learning the newspaper business; she built resilience into every aspect of the operation. She developed multiple revenue streams, invested in talent development, and created systems that could weather both business and political storms.

One of the most important aspects of systematic resilience is having a support network. I tell leaders to identify the five people they can call at any hour of the day. These aren't just friends, they're your resilience team. Think about that for a minute: who are your 2 a.m. phone calls? Who can you turn to when you need perspective, or guidance, or just someone to listen? If you don't have someone, it's time to make an adjustment and make this a priority.

In the modern world, we can even add AI tools to our resilience toolkit. I use ChatGPT sometimes as a thought partner, bouncing ideas off it when I need a different perspective. But remember, these are tools to support your resilience, not replace the human elements.

The key to making all this work is regular assessment. Just like you wouldn't wait six months between checking your car's oil, you shouldn't go for long periods without checking your personal resilience levels. In my family, we do daily check-ins. Sometimes, it's as simple as acknowledging, "I'm just not feeling it today." That honesty itself is a form of resilience.

Here are some of the most common red flags I see in leaders when resilience starts slipping:

- You stop doing the things that used to energize or recharge you
- Minor frustrations feel overwhelming or disproportionate
- You begin pulling away from others and isolating instead of reaching out
- You're constantly exhausted, yet still not sleeping well

If two or more of these hit home, it's time to hit pause, reassess, and make a course correction—before burnout does it for you.

Remember: Resilience isn't about being invulnerable. It's about having systems in place to identify problems early, make necessary adjustments, and keep moving forward. In leadership, as in life, the most sustainable path is usually the one that includes regular maintenance.

Overcoming Imposter Syndrome

I now understand that it was imposter syndrome that made me, after nearly two decades in the Marine Corps, feel insecure about my youth when I had to give that speech in front of more seasoned military personnel in Tampa in 2012. Imposter syndrome is what drove me to focus on appearances rather than substance and consider dying my hair gray to disguise my youth.

I felt nervous as hell when giving my presentation about the Multi-Discipline Intelligence Operators Course, convinced they'd see through me, yet, as I mentioned earlier, several members of the audience came up afterward to congratulate me, praising the program and asking how they could implement it in their commands.

Blinded by imposter syndrome, I failed to realize that most mature professionals care about competence, not cosmetics. I'd wasted energy worrying about how I looked instead of focusing on what I knew and could contribute.

When Admiral Yi Sun-sin was demoted and facing execution due to court politics, he must have felt like an imposter many times. But he focused on his competence, on what he could contribute, rather than on others' perceptions. His resilience in facing these doubts led to him becoming one of history's greatest naval commanders.

Imposter syndrome is not always a bad thing. It keeps us humble, keeps us learning. The danger comes when we let it paralyze us or make us focus on the wrong things, like me with that hair dye.

I recently spoke at Space Command, and before going on stage, I caught myself struggling with some of those same doubts. But instead of trying to look or act a certain way, I focused on what I could contribute. The result? One of the best presentations of my career.

And here's something else I've learned: Imposter syndrome often hits hardest when you're doing something right, when you're pushing beyond your comfort zone. If you're never feeling like an imposter, you might not be challenging yourself enough.

Building Support Systems

I've learned that resilience isn't a solo sport. And in today's rapidly changing world, having a strong support system is more crucial than ever.

Recently, my cousin called me about the death of his brother, a young man in his early thirties who'd passed from brain cancer. During that conversation, we talked about their father, my uncle, who's also battling cancer. The heartbreaking part? My father never once reached out to either his brother or his nephew. He never sent a card, never made a call, never checked in to see how they were doing.

This might seem like a sad family story, but it taught me something crucial about leadership and resilience: You need people who will show up for you, and you need to show up for others. It's not just about having supporters, it's about being part of a support system. You, too, can learn from your own difficult and painful experiences and choose a different path.

In my own career, I've found support in unexpected places. It can be a formal mentor relationship, like with General Bob Neller who gave me honest feedback when I needed it. Or maybe it's peers who understand exactly what you're going through. Or it could even be technology, similar to how I use AI tools as thought partners. But here's what's critical: you must build these support systems before you need them. I learned this lesson early in my military career. When you're in combat, you don't have time to build trust; you need to have it already established. The same principle applies to leadership resilience. You can't surge trust.

I've seen too many leaders try to go it alone, thinking they need to have all the answers. That's a recipe for burnout. Even the most resilient leaders need sounding boards, people who can tell them when they're off track, and spaces where they can be vulnerable.

Resilient Leadership in Action

As we wrap up this exploration of resilience in leadership, I want to stress that resilience isn't about being unbreakable. It's about having the systems in place to recover, rebuild, and keep moving forward.

Ethical leadership works the same way. It's not about being flawless, it's about knowing how to reset when you are off course. When I've fallen short, the most powerful thing I've done is own it quickly, clearly, and without deflection. That's what keeps credibility intact—not perfection, but responsibility.

Think back to where we started, with that story about "kidnapping" four Marines. It wasn't just about making a bold decision; it was about having the resilience to handle the consequences, to stand by that decision, and to turn a potential crisis into an opportunity for building trust and loyalty.

Throughout my career, from that skinny kid in boot camp to leading at the highest levels of military intelligence, I've learned that resilience comes in many forms. Sometimes it's physical, like battling back from injury. Sometimes it's mental, like overcoming imposter syndrome. Sometimes it's professional, like adapting to rapid changes in your field. But always, always, it's about having the right foundations in place.

Remember what we discussed about the personal oil check? That's not just a cute metaphor, it's a survival tool. In today's fast-paced leadership environment, you can't wait for problems to become crises before addressing them. You need to be checking your levels daily, making adjustments, and staying ahead of potential breakdowns.

I look at leaders like Admiral Yi Sun-sin, General Ridgway, Katherine Graham or Ernest Shackleton, who faced seemingly impossible challenges, and I see a common thread: they didn't just persevere blindly. They built systems, created support networks, and maintained their fundamental resilience even in the face of overwhelming odds.

The world isn't getting any simpler. Technology is advancing exponentially, global challenges are becoming more complex, and the demands on leaders are increasing daily. But here's the good news: the basic principles of resilience haven't changed. Take care of your foundations. Build strong support systems. Face your doubts honestly. Keep checking your personal oil levels.

And here's the most important thing I've learned about resilience: it's contagious. When you demonstrate resilience as a leader—not by pretending to be invulnerable but by showing how to handle challenges with grace and systematic approach—you give your team permission to be resilient too.

That's why I'm so open about my own struggles, from the back injury that almost ended my career to my moments of imposter syndrome. Not because I want sympathy, but because I want to show that resilience isn't about avoiding challenges, it's about having a system to work through them.

As you move forward in your leadership journey, remember this: Resilience isn't a destination, it's a daily practice. It's about building the habits, systems, and relationships that will sustain you through challenges. It's about understanding that stress can be a gift when properly managed, that support isn't a weakness, and that even the toughest leaders need to check their oil regularly.

The next chapter will explore how to navigate moral dilemmas in leadership, but you can't make ethical decisions under pressure if you haven't built the resilience to stand firm in your values. That's why this foundation of resilience is so crucial to everything that follows.

In the end, resilience isn't just about surviving, it's about thriving through challenges. It's about building something stronger than what existed before. Because in leadership, as in life, it's not about whether you get knocked down. It's about having the systems in place to get back up, learn from the experience, and keep moving forward.

That's what resilient leadership looks like in action. That's what we should all be striving for.

Looking ahead to Chapter 9, we'll explore the ethical compass that guides our decisions as leaders. But remember—your ethical compass is only as reliable as your resilience to follow it, even when the path gets difficult.

And here's the truth: Your values only matter when they're tested. Anyone can hold a moral compass when skies are clear. But when the storm hits, when the pressure mounts, when it costs you something—that's when resilience becomes the foundation your integrity stands on. Without resilience, even good people bend under pressure. That's why this chapter isn't just about staying strong, it's about staying grounded.

At a certain point in leadership, you stop being seen as a person and start being seen as a title, a rank, a role. You're the job, not the human behind it. People rarely ask how you're doing, and when they do, it's often in passing, without pause or genuine concern.

I remember attending an Air Force promotion ceremony for a Senior Master Sergeant being promoted to Chief. If you've ever been to an Air Force promotion, you know you had better clear your schedule because it's going to take a while. In contrast, in the Marine Corps, we keep it short: report to your commander and Sergeant Major, pin on the new rank, and you're out. It rarely takes more than a minute.

On that day, though, I wasn't really present. Right after the ceremony, I headed home to pick up our oldest English Bulldog, Maxx, to take him to the vet for the last time. He'd been struggling with pain and breathing in the thin Colorado Springs air. The time had come.

I stayed at the ceremony because it was the right thing to do. After congratulating the new Chief and saying my hellos, I left quietly. I went home, gathered the family to say goodbye, and then drove alone with Maxx to the vet. On that ride, I remembered every good moment we'd had: his little loving hop when we came home, how he'd press himself next to us just to be close.

I have had seven combat deployments. I've lost teammates and delivered eulogies. But I can't remember ever crying—not as a teenage Marine, not as a grown man. Not once. Until that day. In the private room the vet gave me, Maxx passed in my arms, and I broke down.

Afterwards, I cleaned up, went back to work, and got on with the day.

Later, outside my home, my neighbor, Space Force CMSgt John Bentivegna, saw me and asked how I was doing. Not in passing. Not to be polite. He stopped, and he meant it. He just listened. No advice. No "stay strong." Just presence.

And that moment—that small but genuine check-in from a peer and a friend—was exactly what I needed. Maybe that's why John went on to become the Chief Master Sergeant of the Space Force. Because sometimes, resilience doesn't come from a system or a strategy. It comes from someone who believes in you when you've forgotten how to believe in yourself.

CHAPTER TAKEAWAYS

- Resilience is a proactive discipline, not a reactive response—prepare for challenges before they arrive
- True resilience requires regular self-assessment through a systematic "personal oil check" of your fundamental systems
- Imposter syndrome often signals growth—learn to use it as feedback rather than letting it paralyze you
- Build your support network before you need it—identify and nurture relationships with people who will tell you both what you want to hear and what you need to hear

---

Resilience Audit:

- Have I identified my five-person support team?
- When was the last time I checked my physical and mental routines?
- What system do I have for regular stress-testing myself and my team?
- Am I building financial, emotional, and relational reserves for the future?
- When did I last grow from and not just survive a challenge?

*"The time is always right
to do what is right."
— Martin Luther King, Jr.*

— 9 —

THE ETHICAL COMPASS: NAVIGATING MORAL DILEMMAS IN LEADERSHIP

I sat in a closed congressional hearing, watching my boss navigate one of the most complex ethical challenges I've faced in my career. The issue was Section 702, an intelligence collection authority that came about after 9/11. Section 702 of the Foreign Intelligence Surveillance Act (FISA) authorizes the U.S. intelligence community to collect foreign intelligence information from non-U.S. persons located outside the United States with the compelled assistance of U.S. communication service providers.

The media narrative had spun this into "NSA is reading everyone's emails," which wasn't just wrong, it was impossible. But here we were, facing Congress, with my boss having to explain something incredibly nuanced in a diplomatic way.

What I witnessed that day was a masterclass in ethical leadership.

He didn't push for or against the authority. Instead, he laid out the facts with absolute clarity. He said, in so many words, that if the United States, through our elected leadership, wants the National Security Agency to have this capability, here's why we need it and here's how we'll use it. You're our elected leaders—the decision is yours.

That moment crystallized something I've learned over three decades of service: The hardest leadership challenges aren't about choosing between right and wrong. They're about navigating between competing "rights"—security versus transparency, individual privacy versus collective safety, speed versus thoroughness. These are the kinds of ethical dilemmas that define modern leadership.

What makes this even harder is that these dilemmas often show up quietly—without warning, headlines, or time to prepare. They're the unexpected calls, the personnel issues no one sees coming, or the funding decision that impacts a partner you genuinely respect. I've had to choose between rewarding loyalty and making a strategic shift that felt necessary for growth. Those decisions don't come with checklists. They come with weight.

I call them *ethical tensions*—not because one side is clearly better, but because both sides hold legitimate weight. Take my work with S2-Stalker Solutions. Every day, I wrestle with what I've come to think of as *dueling duties*: the drive to scale and dominate our industry versus the loyalty I feel toward the people and partnerships that helped me get here. There's no villain in that scenario, no obvious bad choice. Just two worthy paths pulling in different directions.

In these moments, I find myself at a kind of *moral crossroads*. Do I double down on values like loyalty and gratitude? Or do I push forward, fueled by ambition and the belief that growth creates opportunity for everyone involved? Competing virtues, that's what they are—strengths that don't always coexist easily.

I'm sharing this because I think more leaders need to admit that we don't always face clear-cut moral terrain. Often, it's *values in tension.* And the truth is, you can't follow both roads at once. Leadership means choosing. Not between right and wrong, but between right and right. And leadership means owning that choice.

In this chapter, we're going to explore how to develop your ethical compass—not just for the big moments of congressional testimony, but for all the small decisions that build trust and shape culture along the way. Because here's what I know for sure: Your team's willingness to follow you through difficult times isn't built during the crisis, it's built in all the moments leading up to it.

It starts with staying true to your true north—your moral compass, your core values, whatever term resonates. The name doesn't matter. What matters is that you never lose sight of it. Because once you compromise your integrity, it's not something you can patch up and fix later. Trust is earned over time, but when it's gone, it's gone. And so is your credibility.

Sometimes, staying aligned with your values means making hard choices like stepping away from a job, walking away from relationships, or being willing to stand alone. But character is forged in those moments. You don't become a person of integrity by accident, you become one by consistent action, especially when it's inconvenient. As I often say: Return the shopping cart. Whether it's raining, cold, dark, or no one's watching—return the cart. Not because someone told you to, but because that's who you are.

This may be the most important point in the entire book. Leadership is built on trust. Trust is built on integrity. And integrity lives in the smallest of actions, long before the spotlight ever hits you.

The Power of Moral Courage

On December 17, 2010, a Tunisian street vendor named Mohamed Bouazizi reached his breaking point. All he wanted was to sell fruit and vegetables—just enough to support his family and live with dignity. But what he got instead was relentless harassment from local authorities. They confiscated his goods, humiliated him in public, and refused to hear his pleas. That day, after yet another degrading encounter with the police in the town of Sidi Bouzid, Bouazizi walked to the center of the street, doused himself in fuel, and set himself on fire.

His act of self-immolation wasn't just a cry of despair, it was a spark that ignited a revolution. Protests erupted across Tunisia, fueled by long-simmering frustration with government corruption, repression, and economic injustice. Less than a month later, President Zine El Abidine Ben Ali was forced to flee the country. And what started with Bouazizi spread like wildfire. His final act lit the fuse for the Arab Spring—a wave of uprisings and revolutions across the Arab world that reshaped the region and reverberated around the globe.[50]

That single act of desperate moral protest, captured on video and shared across social media, proved more powerful than any weapon, leading to the overthrow of multiple governments and fundamentally reshaping several nations. While I'm certainly not advocating self-immolation as a solution, Bouazizi's story illustrates something profound about moral courage: Sometimes one person standing up and saying "Enough" can change everything.

The ripple effects of Bouazizi's action spread far beyond Tunisia. Within months, protests erupted across the Middle East and North Africa. Regimes that had seemed immovable for decades suddenly found themselves facing existential challenges. Some fell quickly; others responded with brutal crackdowns. The outcomes weren't always positive; in fact, some countries ended up worse off. But that's not really the point. The point is that one person's moral stand, their refusal to accept injustice any longer, catalyzed change on a scale that armies couldn't achieve.

I see this same spirit of moral courage playing out today in Iran, where women are risking their lives to challenge oppressive regulations about how they dress and behave. When Mahsa Amini was murdered by the "morality police" for not wearing her hijab properly, it sparked nationwide protests that continue despite brutal repression. These women know they face imprisonment, torture, even death, yet they continue.[51] That's courage in its purest form.

This kind of courage isn't always about dramatic public stands. Sometimes it's quieter, more personal. I think about Rosa Parks, whose refusal to give up her bus seat wasn't some spontaneous act of defiance, but a carefully considered moral decision that helped ignite the Civil Rights Movement of the 1960s. She knew exactly what she was doing and what it might cost her.

That's an important point about moral courage: it's not about blind rebellion or emotional reactions. It's about making conscious choices to stand up for what's right, even when—especially when—

there's a personal cost. And yes, that cost can feel steep in the short term. You might lose opportunities, relationships, or comfort. But over the long haul, something far more valuable takes shape: your reputation. When you consistently choose principle over convenience, people come to know you as someone who can't be bought. Someone whose name stands for character, for professionalism, and for integrity that doesn't bend with the wind.[52]

In my thirty years of service, I've never faced anything approaching that level of moral challenge. Most of us won't. But these extreme examples illuminate something crucial about ethical leadership—it's not about waiting for the perfect moment or having all the answers. It's about being willing to stand up for what's right, even when it costs you something.

I learned this lesson early in my career when I had to make a decision about reporting a superior officer's misconduct. It wasn't anything approaching life or death, but it felt massive at the time. I knew reporting it could hurt my career, but staying silent would make me complicit. What made the decision possible wasn't some grand moral philosophy, it was all the small ethical choices I'd made leading up to that moment.

Moral courage is like a muscle—it grows stronger with use. Each time you choose to do the right thing, even in small matters, you build your capacity to handle bigger challenges. When you consistently choose integrity over convenience, truth over comfort, right over easy, you're developing the moral strength you'll need when facing real ethical dilemmas.

This is especially crucial in today's world, where social media can amplify courage, cowardice, and convenience. We've seen how quickly moral stands can go viral and inspire others to action. But we've also seen how easily people can be silenced by fear of online backlash or cancel culture. Real moral courage often means being willing to stand alone, to speak up when others stay silent, to do what's right even when it's unpopular.

Building an Ethical Framework

Let's talk about something that's sorely lacking in today's leadership landscape: a clear ethical framework for making tough decisions. Not just rules and regulations—we've got plenty of those—but a genuine moral compass that guides your actions even when nobody's watching.

I recently consulted with a company that had an impressive 50-page ethics manual. Every scenario you could imagine was covered in meticulous detail. But when I asked the employees about real ethical challenges they faced, it became clear that all those rules weren't helping them navigate the gray areas of daily decision-making.

Here's what I've learned: An ethical framework isn't about having answers to every possible scenario. It's about having principles that help you find answers. Let me break down what I believe are the essential elements.

First, there's empathy, and I'm not talking about some soft, feel-good concept. I'm talking about the kind of empathy that makes you a more effective leader. Imagine you have an employee who's already used their two weeks of vacation, and in December, their mother passes away. By the book, they're out of time off. But an empathetic leader finds a way to make it work, not just because it's kind, but because it's right.

The best leaders I've known have this kind of practical empathy. They understand that rules without humanity create a culture of robots, where people do the bare minimum and nothing more. When you show genuine empathy, when you treat people like humans and not resources, they'll move mountains for the team. It's what I think of as the platinum rule: it's not that I treat others how *I* want to be treated but I treat others how *they* want to be treated. This gets to the core of empathy and emotional intelligence. It's not grossly different from the golden rule, but it has a crucial shift in perspective.

That's one reason I've always disliked the term "human resources." It reduces people to a commodity, something to be managed or extracted, rather than honored as the core of any successful organization. I prefer alternatives that reflect how vital people truly are—terms like People Operations, Human Capital & Culture, Talent & Organizational Development, or People & Performance. These aren't just trendy titles. They're reminders that culture, growth, and performance start with how we see people—and how we treat them.

Next comes transparency, which is trickier than it sounds. I learned this lesson at the Defense Intelligence Agency. You've got to be clear about what you can share and what you can't, and why. Simon Sinek talks about "starting with why." I call it "providing context." Instead of just telling your team "Be here at 4 a.m. next week," you explain: "We've got a major end-of-year review, and we need the early start to prepare properly. We'll finish by noon, and this directly impacts your annual bonuses."

This kind of transparency builds trust. But—and this is crucial—it has to be consistent. You can't be transparent only when it's convenient. In ethical leadership, you need a similar framework for deciding what to share, when to share it, and how to share it.

Then there is fairness, and this is where a lot of leaders get tripped up. They confuse being fair with treating everyone exactly the same. That's not fairness, that's laziness. True fairness means understanding that different people need different things to succeed, while maintaining consistent standards for performance and behavior.

I've seen leaders tie themselves in knots trying to be "fair" by treating everyone identically, ignoring the fact that their team members are individuals with different strengths, challenges, and capacities. Real fairness isn't about identical treatment; it's about making sure everyone has what's necessary to meet the same high standards. That doesn't mean giving people everything they ask for. It means equipping them with the tools, support, and clarity required to do the job well. Fairness isn't about comfort, it's about capability.

But here's the piece that ties it all together: accountability. Without accountability, all the empathy, transparency, and fairness in the world don't matter. And I'm seeing a dangerous trend in today's workplace: a reluctance to hold people accountable.

Maybe it's a post-COVID-19 hangover. Maybe it's fear of conflict. Maybe it's a growing belief that accountability somehow conflicts with empathy. Whatever the reason, it's creating cultures where mediocrity becomes acceptable and excellence is discouraged. Too many leaders today shy away from the hard work of holding themselves and their teams accountable. They avoid tough conversations, hesitate to address poor performance, and fail to recognize and promote their top talent. But without accountability, standards erode. And when that happens, even your best people start to wonder why they're bothering to give their best at all.

Most ethical failures don't start with a scandal, they start with a shortcut. A missed standard here, a silent excuse there. Over time, convenience replaces conviction. That's how people find themselves one day far from who they thought they were, without ever making one "bad" decision.

Real accountability isn't about micromanaging or calling people out in public. It's about clarity, consistency, and courage. It starts with clearly defined expectations, so your team knows what success looks like. Then it requires consistent follow-through—celebrating those who exceed the standard and addressing those who fall short. And most importantly, it demands that you, as the leader, model it first. When leaders own their mistakes, give credit where it's due, and make tough personnel decisions based on performance and not politics, they set the tone for the entire organization. Accountability isn't the enemy of empathy, it's what makes empathy mean something. Because when people know the standards are real and earned, trust grows. So does excellence.

Think about it: If you've got two employees—one who consistently goes above and beyond, and another who does the bare minimum—and you treat them exactly the same, what message are you sending? You're telling your top performer that their extra effort doesn't matter. You're telling everyone that standards don't really matter.

This is where having a clear ethical framework becomes crucial. It helps you navigate these complex situations with consistency and clarity. It helps you make decisions that might be unpopular in the moment but prove right over time.

Take the example of Gary DePaul,[53] who studied leaders who maintained high ethical standards during the 2008 financial crisis. The ones who succeeded had something in common: they had developed their ethical framework before the crisis hit. They weren't making up their principles on the fly; they had already decided what they stood for and were ready to stand by those decisions even when it cost them.

And that's why I believe in what I call "pre-deciding your integrity." When you know what you stand for ahead of time, it saves you from the hesitation that gets leaders in trouble. In the moment, clarity is a competitive advantage. It gives you the resolve to act before politics, fear, or noise can interfere.

That's what an ethical framework does—it gives you a foundation for making tough calls. It's not about having all the answers. It's about having a consistent approach to finding answers.

Accountability and Trust

Let me tell you something that might be unpopular: Accountability isn't the enemy of compassionate leadership, it's an essential component of it. Here's what I see happening, especially post-COVID-19: You travel to a hotel, and they forget to put towels in your room, so you call down to request them. An hour later, still no towels. Nobody seems to own the problem or feel responsible for solving it. This isn't just about towels; it's a symptom of what happens when we lose accountability in our culture.

In the military, we have a saying: "Standards without enforcement aren't standards, they're suggestions." Now, I'm not advocating for military-style leadership in civilian organizations, but the principle holds true. When you don't hold people accountable to standards, you're effectively lowering those standards as well as lowering your status in the eyes of your employees or team.

I had a situation where one of our top performers—physically fit, a combat veteran, technically brilliant—started showing up late to meetings. Small thing, right? But I knew from experience that these small ethical slips often precede bigger ones. So, I pulled him aside.

The conversation wasn't about punishment. It was about understanding. "I know why you joined this team," I said. "I know what you're capable of. So, help me understand what's going on, because what I'm seeing doesn't match the leader I know you can be."

That's accountability with empathy. It's not about catching people doing something wrong, it's about helping them live up to their potential. It's similar to what we saw with Admiral William McRaven,[54] who transformed Navy SEAL training not by lowering standards but by adding more support and mentorship to help people meet those standards.

Many leaders think accountability is just about correcting negative behavior. But real accountability also means acknowledging and rewarding positive behavior. When someone on your team does the right thing, especially when it's difficult, that needs to be recognized.

There's a powerful phrase I use often: "Reinforce what you want repeated." Ethical behavior thrives in environments where it's noticed, reinforced, and elevated. When a team member flags a potential risk, or refuses to cut a corner others might, that's your chance to set the tone. Celebrate it, not just with a thank-you, but by sharing the *why* behind their decision with the team.

Consider the case of Cynthia Cooper,[55] the WorldCom whistleblower who exposed one of the largest accounting frauds in history. She didn't wake up one morning and suddenly decide to be ethical. She had built a reputation for integrity through countless smaller decisions. When the big moment came, she had both the moral courage and the credibility to act.

This brings us to trust—the currency of leadership. You can't have accountability without trust, and you can't have trust without accountability. They're two sides of the same coin. Your team needs to trust that you'll hold everyone to the same standards, that you'll be fair in your assessments, and that you'll have their backs when they make tough ethical choices.

I've seen organizations try to systematize this through anonymous feedback channels and whistleblower programs. These can be valuable tools, but they're not substitutes for a culture of trust and accountability. And they're certainly not a shield for leadership. A real leader doesn't outsource tough conversations to a hotline; they confront issues head-on by sitting down and talking face-to-face. When I've seen these programs fail, it's usually because there's no transparency in the process. People submit feedback or raise concerns, and then . . . nothing. No communication, no visible changes, no accountability. If people don't see that their voices lead to action, and that leaders are willing to engage personally, those programs become empty gestures.

The solution isn't complicated, but it is challenging. It requires:

- Clear standards that everyone understands
- Consistent enforcement of those standards
- Regular feedback, both positive and constructive

- Transparency about consequences
- Support for those working to improve

But most importantly, it requires leaders who are willing to be held accountable themselves. I tell my teams: "I expect you to hold me accountable too. If you see me failing to live up to our standards, I need to hear about it." As a retired Marine, I've found that one of the most important things I can do is lead by example—starting with myself. That means having the discipline to stay healthy and fit, not because anyone's making me, but because it's part of who I am. To me, physical discipline is a reflection of character. If I'm not willing to hold myself to a high standard in my own life, how can I ask anyone else to do the same?

General Dwight D. Eisenhower understood this principle deeply. On the eve of D-Day, he wrote two notes—one to announce victory, and another, never needed, to take personal responsibility if the operation failed. "If any blame or fault attaches to the attempt, it is mine alone," he wrote. That's ethical leadership. He didn't wait to see how things played out; he pre-decided to own the outcome, no matter what. And that's what we need more of today: leaders who don't just plan for success, but who prepare to shoulder failure with integrity.

This is ownership before such an idea became extreme.

Ethical Decision-Making Under Pressure

When it comes to making ethical decisions under pressure, many leaders focus on the moment of decision rather than the preparation for that moment. It's like expecting to bench press 300 pounds without ever training your muscles. The time to develop your ethical decision-making capacity isn't during the crisis, it's in all the moments leading up to it. This reminds me of two of the Special Operations Forces Truths: Special Operations Forces cannot be mass produced, and competent Special Operations Forces cannot be created after emergencies occur. The same goes for ethical leadership. You can't fake character in a high-stakes moment. You must build it—daily, deliberately, and long before the pressure is on.

In my current role consulting with organizations, I often get asked about whistleblower programs and ethical reporting systems. Leaders want to know how to set them up, what policies to put in place, and how to handle reports. These are good questions, but they're focusing on the wrong end of the problem.

In the Department of Defense, we have the Inspector General system. Anyone can report anything, anytime. Sounds great, right? But here's the problem: there is no transparency in the process. You submit a report, and then . . . silence. Maybe two years later you hear something. Maybe you never hear anything at all. The result? Nobody trusts the system, and thus it provides little value.

Another situation I encountered while at USSC: We had a lieutenant colonel who was removed for being what was termed a "toxic leader." When I heard about it, I was stunned. I'd met her briefly and been incredibly impressed. But somewhere along the line, something went wrong. The tragedy wasn't just that we lost a talented officer, it was that nobody had stepped in earlier to say, "Ma'am, I want you to know how you're being perceived, and this isn't going to play out well if things don't change."

That's the kind of ethical intervention that needs to happen more often. But it only happens in organizations where people feel safe speaking truth to power. As Dov Seidman[56] points out in his research on ethical leadership, the key factor isn't the presence of formal systems, it's the existence of psychological safety that allows people to raise concerns before they become crises.

So how do you build that kind of environment?

First, you need what I call "ethical muscle memory." Just like a Marine practices weapons drills until they become instinct, leaders need to practice ethical decision-making in low-stakes situations until it becomes automatic. Every small choice—whether to take credit for someone else's work, whether to speak up about a minor problem, whether to cut corners to meet a deadline—these are your training opportunities.

Second, you need to create what Amy Edmondson[57] calls "psychological safety"—an environment where people feel safe raising concerns without fear of retaliation. This doesn't mean everyone gets their way or that standards are lowered. It means creating a culture where ethical concerns are treated as valuable intelligence rather than unwelcome disruption.

Think about it this way: In combat, you want your Marines to feel comfortable telling you if they spot something wrong. The same principle applies in any organization. Your people are your ethical early warning system, but only if they trust that speaking up won't get them reprimanded.

Here's a practical framework I use for ethical decision-making under pressure:

- Pause and assess: What are the ethical principles at stake?
- Consider impact: Who will be affected by this decision?

- Examine alternatives: What are all possible courses of action?

- Test your thinking: Would this decision stand up to public scrutiny?

- Make the call: Decide and act with conviction

But here's the crucial part: you have to practice this framework on small decisions so it's available when you face big ones. It's like muscle memory—you don't want to be figuring out how to make ethical decisions when you're already under pressure.

CHAPTER TAKEAWAYS

- Ethical leadership isn't about having all the answers; it's about having a consistent framework for finding answers.

- Real accountability combines high standards with high support; you need both to build an ethical culture.

- Trust and transparency are essential for ethical decision-making, but they must be backed by consistent action.

- The time to develop ethical decision-making capacity is before you need it, through practice with small choices.

- Creating psychological safety is crucial for early detection and prevention of ethical problems.

Remember, your ethical compass isn't just about navigating your own decisions. It's about creating an environment where others can make ethical choices too. Because in the end, leadership isn't just about what you do, it's about what you inspire others to do.

If someone were to ask your team, "What does this leader tolerate? What do they reward? What would they never accept?", would their answers match your values? That's the ethical audit worth doing, because the real measurement of your compass isn't on your wall, it's in their behavior. In the end, the job isn't just to hold the line, it's to *be* the line others measure themselves against.

Ethical Compass Calibration

Ask yourself:

- What's a value I say I believe in but haven't had tested yet?
- When was the last time I made the hard right call instead of the easy wrong one?
- Who do I trust to hold me accountable if I drift?
- Where in my leadership could more transparency or empathy make a difference?
- What behavior am I quietly tolerating that I shouldn't?

"Your time is limited,
so don't waste it living someone else's life."
— Steve Jobs

— CONCLUSION —

YOUR LEADERSHIP JOURNEY BEGINS NOW

The day after my retirement ceremony, I found myself completely unemployed with no house to live in, and my wife and three young daughters piled into our minivan. Where most might feel anxiety or imposter syndrome at this juncture, I felt what I can only describe as authentic confidence.

We embarked on a four-month journey through Montana's national parks, to Mount Rushmore, into Canada, and eventually to Massachusetts to visit my 99-year-old grandmother. All with daughters who were four, two, and one at the time.

This wasn't reckless abandon. It was a deliberate choice to decompress after 31 years of going 100 miles an hour, seven combat tours, and saying goodbye to too many people I loved. I needed space to redefine myself beyond my rank or position in the military.

During one hike slightly off the beaten path, a mountain goat with impossibly white fur photobombed our family selfie. In a small church in Kansas, I found an hour of unexpected solitude and reflection. These moments of peace were exactly what I needed.

I remember my wife spotting our current house on Zillow during this trip. "It has the schools we want, the right temperature, the right cost," she said. I flew out the next day to see it, and our real estate agent turned out to be someone who had worked with me at MARSOC.

Gradually, consulting opportunities and job offers began to materialize. I hadn't searched for them; they simply found me. It was as if stepping away had created the space for new opportunities to enter.

This experience taught me something crucial about leadership: Even the best sports car can only redline for so long. Authentic leadership starts with taking care of yourself. The leadership journey doesn't end; sometimes it just needs a reset.

Real leadership isn't sustained by brute force or constant motion. It's sustained by intention, and intention begins with recovery. That's something I didn't always understand in my younger years but learned deeply in the quiet moments after retirement. Slowing down doesn't mean stepping back from excellence; it means preparing yourself to meet the next moment with clarity, strength, and purpose. You can't pour into others from an empty cup.

Throughout these pages, we've explored the critical steps and mindsets needed before stepping into leadership roles. Now, as we wrap up our journey together, I want to share some final thoughts that will help you integrate everything we've covered and put it into action.

The Five Pillars of Effective Leadership

As you continue your leadership journey, these five foundational pillars will keep you grounded, focused, and effective, no matter your title or terrain. They're not just ideas; they're the habits, mindsets, and values that carry you through both calm and chaos.

1. Clarity of Purpose

Be adaptable but anchored in values.

Great leaders evolve. They adjust to new challenges, new people, and new environments. But adaptability without direction is just drift. What keeps you centered is a clear sense of purpose, built on ethics, discipline, and love for your people and the mission. The world will keep changing; your core can't. When you know what you stand for, decision-making becomes faster, clearer, and stronger. That's how you lead with integrity, not insecurity.

2. Empathy with Accountability

Lead with understanding but hold the standard.

You can't lead people you don't understand. But you also can't build teams if you let standards slide. The best leaders balance empathy with expectation. They connect deeply, but they don't coddle. They coach. This pillar is where love meets clarity, where compassion doesn't cancel accountability, it fuels it. That's how people grow—when they're believed in, stretched, and supported. You want to lead with heart, not just heat.

3. Resilience as a System

Build systems that sustain you through challenge.

Resilience isn't just about being tough, it's about staying ready. It's knowing your limits, doing your "oil checks," and refusing to let small problems become big ones. Whether it's physical health, mental clarity, or emotional control—resilience is a system, not a mood. Your drive is part of that system. So is your routine, your rest, your support network, and your mindset. This is what keeps you going when others burn out.

4. Intentional Influence

Your leadership leaves a ripple—design it on purpose.

Everything you say, do, tolerate, and reward creates culture. So lead like someone is watching, because they are. The ripple effect of your leadership doesn't happen by accident. It's built moment by moment, in hallway conversations, tough calls, and small acts of courage. The key is intentionality: know your vision, model it, and embed it in others. That's how your influence grows, long after you've left the room.

5. Growth Without a Finish Line

There is no graduation date. Leadership is daily.

Leadership isn't a status, it's a responsibility. It requires constant refinement, daily choices, and ongoing commitment to the basics. You never outgrow the fundamentals: humility, preparation, listening, showing up early, being accountable. Titles fade. Character compounds. And the best leaders never stop learning, because they know the moment they think they've "made it," they've already started slipping. Stay sharp. Stay humble. Stay hungry.

The Critical Role of Self-Care in Leadership

One aspect of leadership that often gets overlooked is the fundamental importance of taking care of yourself, both physically and mentally. Having lost too many friends to preventable health issues, I've become increasingly passionate about this topic. As I approach 50, one of the first questions I ask when reconnecting with old colleagues is, "How's your health?" The responses often involve discussions of new surgeries or ongoing health challenges.

Leadership demands energy, resilience, and clarity of mind. You can't provide these if you're not taking care of yourself. This isn't about becoming a fitness fanatic or adopting an extreme lifestyle. Rather, it's about finding sustainable ways to maintain your health and well-being. For me, this has meant exploring various approaches to physical and mental wellness. I've discovered that yoga, surprisingly, has been one of the hardest things I've ever done. But it has taught me valuable lessons about patience, persistence, and the importance of stepping outside my comfort zone.

Building Your Support Network

As you progress in your leadership journey, you'll find that it can become increasingly lonely at the top. This is something I experienced firsthand during my final years in the Marine Corps. When you reach senior positions, finding people who will give you honest feedback becomes more challenging. Everyone wants to tell you what they think you want to hear.

This is why it's crucial to build and maintain relationships with people who will tell you the truth, who will give it to you straight. This might be a spouse, a trusted friend, or a mentor, but it's rarely going to be an employee. The reality is that most people won't risk their job to tell their boss hard truths.

The Power of Long-Term Vision

One of the biggest traps leaders fall into is becoming too focused on short-term wins at the expense of long-term success. I call this the "five-meter target" syndrome, where you're so focused on what's directly in front of you that you lose sight of the bigger picture. The most effective leaders maintain a clear vision of their long-term objectives while managing day-to-day challenges. They understand that sustainable success requires patience, persistence, and the ability to stay focused on what truly matters.

The Importance of Personal Accountability

Let me share something that might seem unrelated at first: I recently set a goal to break 80 in golf by the end of 2025. I've hired a coach, created a detailed plan, and built in specific accountability measures. In fact, I've told my coach that if I don't achieve this goal by December 31, 2025, I'll never play golf again.

Now, you might think that's extreme, and maybe it is. But I've learned that without real accountability, goals often remain just wishful thinking. The same principle applies to leadership development. You need clear objectives, regular feedback, and real consequences to drive meaningful growth.

Embracing the Unknown: Your Leadership Future

As we look ahead to 2025 and beyond, none of us can predict exactly what challenges and opportunities await. The pace of change continues to accelerate, whether it's artificial intelligence, geopolitical shifts, or evolving workplace dynamics. But here's what I know for certain: The fundamentals of leadership we have discussed in this book will remain crucial.

You've made it this far in the book, which tells me something: you care about getting leadership right. Not by accident. Not by luck. But by design. If you're carrying doubts right now . . . good. Doubt is your body's way of reminding you to prepare, to sharpen, to put in the work. I've felt it too, more times than I can count. But here's the truth: You are more capable than you think. And you don't have to figure this out alone. This book was written to be your guide—not for the rank you wear today, but for the leader you're becoming.

A Final Personal Note

Leadership is about making consistent choices that positively influence others, even when it's challenging or uncomfortable. It's about doing the right thing, not because someone is watching, but because it's right. It's about preparing yourself today for the leadership opportunities of tomorrow.

One of the most underrated leadership traits is the ability to pause. Not to freeze, not to stall, but to deliberately pause, reflect, and respond rather than react. In a world that rewards speed and noise, the leader who pauses gains clarity, protects their integrity, and makes decisions that last. A well-timed pause can prevent a life-long regret.

The journey ahead won't always be easy. There will be setbacks, doubts, and moments of uncertainty. Leadership isn't a medal you wear, it's a mindset you carry. It's the quiet strength behind the hard decisions. It's the call you return when someone needs help. It's showing up early, staying late, and refusing to lower your standards. I've seen titles come and go. But character? That lasts. And the impact you make as a leader isn't always something you'll see— it's something others will feel, long after you've moved on.

A title may give you authority, but it will never guarantee respect. That must be earned through consistency, humility, and presence. Leadership is not a destination, it's a responsibility. One that renews every single day you put on the uniform, walk into the office, or step into your home. People aren't looking for perfection. They're watching for consistency. For someone they can count on. For someone who listens more than they talk and leads more by example than by directive.

But if you stay true to your values, maintain your moral compass, and consistently work on developing yourself, you'll be ready when leadership opportunities present themselves.

Thank you for joining me in this exploration of leadership development. The rest is up to you.

Now get out there and lead. Your future team is waiting. You don't need to be loud to be heard. You need to be real. Leadership doesn't begin at the podium. It starts *Left of Leadership*—in the moments before you're ever given the mic.

From one imperfect leader to another, thank you. Now go lead with heart, clarity, and courage.

— ACKNOWLEDGMENTS —

Bringing "Left of Leadership" to fruition has been a journey shaped by incredible support, insightful critique, and unwavering belief from many. This book, much like leadership itself, is truly a collaborative effort.

My deepest gratitude goes to my writing team: Holly Hudson, Charles Levin, and Lily Drew. Your unwavering support, invaluable advice, and countless emails and calls along this journey are the reason this book exists today.

I am also deeply grateful to individuals whose words and actions provided profound inspiration and encouragement throughout this endeavor. To Audie Cooper, who often reminded me that we all have at least one book in us, and to Robert Irvine, who continually encouraged me to pursue my goals—your belief meant the world.

To my coach and fellow Marine, J.R. Flatter, thank you for spending invaluable time on the phone with me during my military transition. You coached me for months as I navigated both retirement, moving a family, starting a new business, and guided me through the incredible opportunities I have received and expect to earn.

Michael Quinn—thank you for telling me what I needed to hear, not just what I wanted. During my retirement and transition, your friendship, late-night calls, and sage counsel reminded me that relationships outweigh any résumé. I'm deeply grateful for the guidance and clarity you gave when I needed it most.

To my closest friends—Eric Banks, Edwin Tharnish, Michael "Greg" McCormack, Matthew Croy, Christopher Lloyd, Brian Singer, Stuart Tong, & Ken Pinckard—the few I initially confided in about this endeavor, thank you for your candid feedback on everything from the cover and title to the substance of my stories. Your honesty was invaluable.

And to three gentlemen that I strive to be more like and pause everything I'm doing when there's the chance to speak or respond to a text from: Phil Chudoba (Col USMC ret), Keith Lawless (Col USMC ret), and Robert "Bob" Sharp (VADM USN ret). I've told you three before, and I mean this, if I could be anything, I'd be more like you—the finest we have, true gentlemen.

This book draws heavily on the lessons of leadership, and for that, I am eternally indebted to the senior leaders I was afforded the immense opportunity to work for and learn from. To Col Richard Martin USMC, Col George Bristol (USMC ret), Col J. Darren Duke (USMC ret), LtGen (USMC ret) Vince Stewart, LTG (USA ret) Robert Ashley, ADM (USN ret) Michael Rogers, GEN (USA ret) Paul Nakasone, Gen (USSF ret) John "Jay" Raymond, and GEN (USA ret) James "Jim" Dickinson—serving by your side did more than just offer an insight into the national security apparatus; it granted me unprecedented clarity into its complexities, its critical challenges, and its transformative opportunities; and it afforded me the opportunity to earn a PhD in leadership simply by being in your presence.

A special and profound thank you to GEN (USA ret.) Paul Nakasone for writing the powerful endorsement for this book, but more importantly, for being the epitome of the type of leader I aspire to be. I could not be more grateful to have served alongside you and to call you a friend today.

To my Grandma "Nana" Anna Gallagher, who is so tough she moved from Florida back to Massachusetts and still today, at 99, always tells me how proud she is of me and how proud her George, my Grandpa would be. I love you, Nana!

And to the United States Marine Corps. You took a boy and made a man. Whatever I am or will become professionally will always come second to the title I earned—Marine. Semper Fidelis!

Lastly, and with all my heart, to my wife Malerie and my three amazing girls, Olivia, Grace, and Scarlett—your unwavering love and boundless support have completed what the Marine Corps built and have helped to make me the leader, husband, and father I am today. I love you.

— NOTES —

1 Stockdale, James B., and Sybil Stockdale. In Love and War: The Story of a Family's Ordeal and Sacrifice During the Vietnam Years. New York: Harper & Row, 1984.

2 Stockdale, James B. "Courage Under Fire: Testing Epictetus's Doctrines in a Laboratory of Human Behavior." Stanford: Hoover Institution Press, 1993, pp. 23-26.

3 Collins, Jim. Good to Great: Why Some Companies Make the Leap...And Others Don't. New York: Harper Business, 2001, pp. 83-85. The term "Stockdale Paradox" is explained in detail in Chapter 4.

4 Stockdale, James B. Thoughts of a Philosophical Fighter Pilot. Stanford: Hoover Institution Press, 1995, pp. 124-129.

5 Rochester, Stuart I., and Frederick Kiley. Honor Bound: American Prisoners of War in Southeast Asia, 1961-1973. Naval Institute Press, 1999, pp. 308-315.

6 Small, Hugh. "Florence Nightingale: Avenging Angel." London: Constable, 1998.

7 McDonald, Lynn. "Florence Nightingale: An Introduction to Her Life and Family." Waterloo: Wilfrid Laurier University Press, 2001.

8 Cohen, I. Bernard. "Florence Nightingale." Scientific American 250, no. 3 (1984).

9 Magnello, Eileen. "Victorian Statistical Graphics and the Iconography of Florence Nightingale's Polar Area Graphs." Victorian Review 45, no. 2 (2019).

10 Bostridge, Mark. "Florence Nightingale: The Woman and Her Legend." London: Viking, 2008.

11 Keith, Judith. "Florence Nightingale: Statistician and Consultant Epidemiologist." International Nursing Review 35, no. 5 (1988).

12 Here's the list: I'm #1614 https://www.mid.ru/ru/maps/us/1814243/.

13 Frankl, Viktor E. Man's Search for Meaning. Boston: Beacon Press, 2006 (originally published 1946).

14 Potter, E.B., Nimitz. Annapolis: Naval Institute Press, 1976.

15 Buell, Thomas B., Master of Sea Power: A Biography of Fleet Admiral Chester W. Nimitz. Annapolis: Naval Institute Press, 1991.

16 Lord, Walter, Incredible Victory: The Battle of Midway. New York: Harper & Row, 1967.

17 Stacy Schiff, A Great Improvisation: Franklin, France, and the Birth of America (New York: Henry Holt, 2005.

18 Walter Isaacson, Benjamin Franklin: An American Life (New York: Simon & Schuster, 2003).

19 Gordon S. Wood, The Americanization of Benjamin Franklin (New York: Penguin Press, 2004).

20 Schiff, A Great Improvisation.

21 Isaacson, Benjamin Franklin: An American Life.

22 Mary Ann Glendon, A World Made New: Eleanor Roosevelt and the Universal Declaration of Human Rights (New York: Random House, 2001).

23 Blanche Wiesen Cook, Eleanor Roosevelt, Volume 3: The War Years and After, 1939-1962 (New York: Viking, 2016).

24 Allida Black, Casting Her Own Shadow: Eleanor Roosevelt and the Shaping of Postwar Liberalism (New York: Columbia University Press, 1996).

25 Jason Berger, A New Deal for the World: Eleanor Roosevelt and American Foreign Policy (New York: Columbia University Press, 1981).

26 Glendon, A World Made New, 150-152.

27 David Emblidge, ed., My Day: The Best of Eleanor Roosevelt's Acclaimed Newspaper Columns, 1936-1962 (New York: Da Capo Press, 2001).

28 Allida Black, "Eleanor Roosevelt and the Universal Declaration of Human Rights," OAH Magazine of History 22, no. 2 (2008).

29 Cook, Eleanor Roosevelt, 401-403.

30 Joseph P. Lash, Eleanor: The Years Alone (New York: Norton, 1972).

31 Greg Behrman, The Most Noble Adventure: The Marshall Plan and the Time When America Helped Save Europe (New York: Free Press, 2007).

32 David M. Oshinsky, A Conspiracy So Immense: The World of Joe McCarthy (New York: Oxford University Press, 2005).

33 Michael J. Hogan, The Marshall Plan: America, Britain, and the Reconstruction of Western Europe, 1947-1952 (Cambridge: Cambridge University Press, 1987).

34 Behrman, The Most Noble Adventure, 156-158.

35 Ellen Schrecker, Many Are the Crimes: McCarthyism in America (Princeton: Princeton University Press, 1998).

36 Oshinsky, A Conspiracy So Immense, 503-505.

37 John Gimbel, The Origins of the Marshall Plan (Stanford: Stanford University Press, 1976).

38 Richard H. Rovere, Senator Joe McCarthy (New York: Harper & Row, 1959).

39 Ha, Tae-hung, trans. Imjin Changch'o: Admiral Yi Sun-sin's Memorials to Court. Republic of Korea: Yonsei University Press, 1981.

40 Kim, Zae-geun. "Admiral Yi Sun-sin's Leadership and Ethical Standards." Journal of Military History 62.4 (2016).

41 Park, Yune-hee. Admiral Yi and His Turtle Ship Armada. Seoul: Hanjin Publishing Co., 1978.

42 Turnbull, Stephen. Samurai Invasion: Japan's Korean War 1592-1598. London: Cassell & Co., 2002.

43 Choi, Min-ho. "Lessons in Strategic Leadership: Admiral Yi Sun-sin's Legacy in Modern Management." International Journal of Leadership Studies 23.2.

44 Rees, David. Korea: The Limited War. New York: St. Martin's Press, 1964.

45 Blair, Clay. The Forgotten War: America in Korea 1950-1953. New York: Times Books, 1987.

46 Ridgway, Matthew B. The Korean War. Garden City, NY: Doubleday.

47 Graham, Katharine. Personal History. New York: Alfred A. Knopf, 1997.

48 Bradlee, Benjamin C. A Good Life: Newspapering and Other Adventures. New York: Simon & Schuster, 1995.

49 Halberstam, David. The Powers That Be. New York: Alfred A. Knopf.

50 Gelvin, James L. "The Arab Uprisings: What Everyone Needs to Know." Oxford University Press, 2012. pp. 26-28.

51 Azadeh, Moaveni. "The Protests in Iran Have Shaken the Islamic Republic to Its Core." Time Magazine, October 13, 2023.

52 Theoharis, Jeanne. "The Rebellious Life of Mrs. Rosa Parks." Beacon Press, 2013, pp. 62-64.

53 DePaul, Gary W. "Nine Practices of 21st Century Leadership: A Guide for Inspiring Creativity, Innovation, and Engagement." CRC Press, 2015, pp. 142-146.

54 McRaven, William H. "Sea Stories: My Life in Special Operations." Grand Central Publishing, 2019, pp. 341-344.

55 Cooper, Cynthia. "Extraordinary Circumstances: The Journey of a Corporate Whistleblower." John Wiley & Sons, 2008.

56 Seidman, Dov. "How: Why HOW We Do Anything Means Everything." Wiley, 2021, pp. 192-195.

57 Edmondson, Amy C. "The Fearless Organization: Creating Psychological Safety in the Workplace for Learning, Innovation, and Growth." Wiley, 2018, pp. 88-92.

— ABOUT THE AUTHOR —

Scott H. Stalker is a combat-proven leader and nationally respected expert in intelligence, space operations, cybersecurity, national security, and leadership. Over more than 30 years in the United States Marine Corps, he held some of the most senior enlisted positions in the Department of Defense.

Born in Lebanon, New Hampshire and raised in the Bay Area of California, Scott enlisted in the Marine Corps at the age of 17, launching a career defined by service, grit, and forward-thinking leadership.

He made history as the first and only Marine to serve as the Command Senior Enlisted Leader (CSEL) for U.S. Cyber Command, U.S. Space Command, and the Defense Intelligence Agency. He also served as the CSEL for the National Security Agency and as the Intelligence Chief for Marine Corps Forces Special Operations Command (MARSOC).

His operational experience includes seven combat tours, including deployments to Mogadishu, Somalia; Bosnia; and multiple tours in Iraq. He also supported non-combatant evacuation operations in Tirana, Albania, and participated in command visits to Afghanistan, bringing a wealth of real-world insight to the principles of leadership and decision-making under pressure.

Today, Scott lives with his family in the Wilmington, North Carolina area, where he leads his Veteran-Owned Small Business, S-2 Stalker Solutions LLC, providing strategic support to the U.S. Government. He also advises leaders and organizations across sectors and delivers keynote speeches on leadership and national security.

You can contact the author directly at his website:
www.stalkersolutions.com

Left of Leadership is the culmination of a lifetime spent on the front lines of strategy, service, and leadership.

www.ingramcontent.com/pod-product-compliance
Lightning Source LLC
Chambersburg PA
CBHW071325120626
46546CB00002B/445